The Ghosts of Cape May

BOOK 3

1st Edition

Craig McManus

© ChannelCraig, Inc.

The Ghosts of Cape May Book 3

Copyright © 2008 by ChannelCraig, Inc.

All rights reserved. This book, or parts thereof, may not be reproduced in any form without written permission from the publisher.

Story Editors: Kathy DeLuccia & Willy Kare

First Edition: May 2008

ISBN13   978-0-9785444-2-3

Front cover: Something plays the phantom organ at the Physick Estate

Photography by
Maciek Nabrdalik

To Kathy DeLuccia

My dearest friend and guiding light

Contents

Introduction 10

Return to The Physick Estate 18

The Parris Cottage 30

The Bacchus Inn 46

The Linda Lee 54

The Jacob Leaming House 76

Ludlam House 86

The Carroll Villa 116

The Virginia Hotel 128

Ghosts of the West — West Cape May 134

The Albert Stevens Inn 140

The Wilbraham Mansion 158

Highland House 174

Eldredge House 194

The Old Yellow House on Eldredge Avenue 212

Flanegan Art & Framing 226

The Old Reeves Homestead 242

The Ghosts of Higbee Beach 266

Ghosts of the Lighthouse 276

Introduction

Whoever thought Cape May was *this* haunted? When I first wrote *The Ghosts of Cape May Book 1*, I fantasized about finding so many haunts in town that I would need to write three volumes. I thought I had discovered most of this historic seaside resort's bumps in the night, but I was wrong, and I went on to write *Book 2*. As the two books gained popularity and I began to develop the ghost trolley tours with the Mid-Atlantic Center for the Arts (MAC,) I noticed something started to change. People who never had discussed having ghosts were now openly broaching the subject with not just me, but with their guests! While some people will always be afraid to talk about ghosts, most people find the subject intriguing, and Cape May was finally realizing one of its best hidden assets: ghosts. The ectoplasmic tide had turned and the "Ghosts Welcome" sign was proudly hung throughout town.

Now before we get carried away, let me clearly state that the town did not just recently become haunted. It's always been haunted and probably always *will* be haunted. The living love Cape May. We die, we still love Cape May. If Cape May is purgatory, count me in for a timeshare!

There are many subtleties to hauntings. In these pages, you will see that not every haunting is the same and many go unnoticed. What most people think of as a ghost experience or a classic haunting, only happens in Hollywood or on the pages of sensationalist paranormal websites. True ghost stories are absolutely fascinating, defying everything we have been taught in school and making us wonder what really is beyond the four walls around us. I have tried to include the most unique investigations in these pages. I am going to bring you up close to the ghosts. You will come right along with me in these pages as I investigate each haunt. It's alright to be afraid, just be prepared to learn and experience something completely new and exciting that will allow you to come away from this third book with a new understanding of ghosts.

I have been fascinated with ghosts and hauntings since I was a teenager. At first, I too was frightened at the thought that anything else with a mind and personality could be existing with us without our knowing

about it. I grew up having an over-active imagination, aggravated by latent psychic and mediumistic abilities, coupled with a childhood fear of the unknown, plus depression, that stemmed from a worry based gene pool—that I happened to be stuck with. I often joke that I could be the poster boy for Paxil.®

Instead, I chose a different path. I now look at the universe as a much bigger place and keep reminding myself that we are not alone, even here on Earth. We just can't control everything around us, and sometimes we need to let go of human control issues. And we do.

Ghosts exist, they have always been here. They were once people or animals or some form of living being. We have termed them "dead" because they are no longer like us, but they have not stopped "living." They have moved on to another form of existence, which is some other version of ourselves made up of an energy we rarely see or hear and can sometimes measure with our current equipment. Oh yes, we *do* see, hear or feel something, but that is usually when a ghost's energy interacts with our energy, by a conscious effort on the ghost's part or by complete accident. Ghosts exist all around us in life, but most of the time they *do not* interact with us at all. It's when they do interact that the fun begins.

In researching the stories for this book, I noticed a pattern developing in some of the hauntings. Many of the players were young children. Adult ghosts may have been in the vicinity, but they did not interact with me and seemed to have no part in the haunting phenomena. In *Book 2*, I have an entire chapter on the Paranormal Playground, about the ghostly children of Cape May. The ratio of children to adults in the ghost realm in Cape May seems to be rather high. Either the adult ghosts want to maintain their privacy and the children are just being children and acting up or Cape May is one big haunted orphanage!

A topic that comes up when I lecture about ghosts and hauntings is getting ghosts to cross over to Heaven. While I am not in the business of getting ghosts to move on. I do try to send *healing light* to wherever I am investigating in hope that a higher power might give any stranded souls a lift. I get told to "butt out" quite a bit by the ghosts. The last thing they want to hear from me is my telling them to leave their homes. The energy I feel I need to put out there is, to quote spy novelist Ian Fleming, "live and let live."

The ghost realm could well be another dimension we all pass through on the way to Heaven. We really don't know. Maybe it is a place where we can look back at our lives and the people we have left behind. Could it also be another dimension in time and space that surrounds our own as naturally as the atmosphere surrounds the Earth. We really do not understand it at all right now. This book is about human-ghost interaction and, specifically, those meetings that take place at America's oldest, and most haunted seaside resort, Cape May.

The queen of the seaside resorts is still reigning after more than 300 years! Cape May has a very special energy — positive energy — that keeps bringing people back for more. I'm talking about the living this time. I recently battled a bad upper respiratory infection, and the only time I felt great the entire week was when I took a long walk along Higbee Beach from Cape May Point. The salt air down there is something special and you can see why history recalls thousands of people coming every summer to walk the flat, firm beaches of cool Cape May. Truly a resort with restorative powers, Cape May has never lost site of its historic roots. The past and the present walk hand in hand in Cape May and being there is like one big disconnect from the stress and distraction of modern living. It's also a great window into past energies!

When I walk the beaches, I can almost see droves of people in Colonial and Victorian dress walking right along side me. You don't see them? Oh that's right, sorry, I keep forgetting I'm a medium.

In this book I will be incorporating more audio findings or EVPs recorded during my investigations. Many of my tapes seems to have EVPs. Some of the recordings even have multiple "ghost voices." People have been recording "Electronic Voice Phenomena" for many years. Are these ghostly sounds, words and bits of dialogue truly communications from the dead? Many paranormal researchers think so.

I rarely paid attention to EVPs in my early investigations. I was more psychic-medium egocentric and felt my *internal* equipment was the best source of data in my investigations. When I started uploading all of my old investigation cassette recordings into Adobe Audition® (a sound editing program) to make them easier to access and catalogue, I realized I was not the only one speaking on the tape. Others were carrying on in the

Cape May's beach circa 1907 — notice the "Palmist" sign on the tent Hmm... I wonder if I was working the beaches back then? (Author's Collection)

background, and the more I listened the more I got sucked into the world of EVP recording.

A fascinating part of EVPs is hearing a ghost directly answering my questions. Most of the time the only response is background talk or an answer that makes absolutely no sense. Words, noises, inaudible voices chatting on about something — but one cannot understand what it is they are saying. Only in a few instances did the ghosts, if that is truly who was being recorded on the tape, give me any kind of facts that helped in the investigation.

I try not to rely on EVPs as the primary source for any investigation. There are still too many unanswered questions about EVPs. We can record these "voices," but we do not understand why we can do it or where the voices are coming from. I add EVP evidence into the mix. My psychic feelings go in first, then the stories of those I interview with their firsthand experiences. Next I weigh in the EVPs. Scientific readings like EMF field and temperature fluctuation will also be noted as a part of the investigation. If the only thing people experience in a house is EVPs, with no other haunting phenomena happening, it does not make for a very interesting investigation. It is rather like sitting and listening to a radio show for hours. No visual, no physical, just noise. Not my cup of psychic tea.

Reviewing the audio tapes from previous investigations was extremely time consuming. At first, I started scanning each pause in dialogue for EVPs. After about ten hours of listening, my brain began to turn to mush from all of the white noise. I abandoned quickly the idea of finding every EVP that I had ever recorded. Reviewing hours of tape for EVPs is one of the most boring, painful things you can ever do to your ears and mind. It is like sitting in a doctor's waiting room for a week reading the same magazine over and over, while listening to the same background chatter. Luckily, I was able to find some great EVPs before I overloaded my neural pathways once and for all!

I hope you enjoy this third book on the ghosts of Cape May. This old seaside town is like a second home to me. There may be flashier resorts and more hip vacation spots, but for those in "the know," Cape May does just fine. It's one of the best vacation spots in the USA to kick back, relax and take in some positive energy.

I did not start the project of cataloging the ghosts of Cape May and I won't be the last to do it—paranormal Cape May is an open book—everyone is welcome to come and experience the ghosts and bring home a few tales for themselves. I keep doing my part to keep the ghosts in Cape May alive and well, at least their stories anyway! I hope my writing sheds some light, and a little humor, on a topic that remains way too scary and serious for too many people. Loosen up folks—the dead don't like stiffs. You gotta enjoy everything life has to offer, even if it happens to be lurking right behind you right now...

Got the book, get the tanning oil, bury yourself in the sand and let's go haunting!

Return to The Physick Estate
METAPHYSICS MEETS THE PHYSICKS
Historic Mansion & Museum - 1048 Washington Street

CALLING Aunt Emilie — Calling Aunt Emilie — I'm *back!* You gotta give the Physick family credit, it's not easy to find good help, when you're dead, and Aunt Emily does a pretty good job of keeping up appearances at the old Emlen Physick Estate mansion with a (pardon the pun) skeleton crew. I go into detail about the mansion in *Book 1*, so I won't rehash a lot of history in this chapter. However, a house this big and active was just ripe for another visit or two from this Medium, and so I decided to pay a visit to Aunt Emilie and the gang one more time.

The Physick Mansion was built in 1879 and has been home to basically one family since then. The house was built by Dr. Emlen Physick and shared by the doctor and his mother, Mrs. Frances M. Ralston and Mrs. Ralston's two sisters, Emilie Parmentier and Isabelle (Bella) Parmentier. Bella suffered from Epilepsy and died in her thirties around 1883, shortly after the family moved in to the new house.

My investigations over the past few years have lead me to believe that both Aunt Emilie and Aunt Bella are haunting the house. Since we began our Historic Haunts trolley tour, which drops people off at the Physick Estate at night and lets them tour the inside of the home, patrons have reported encounters with ghostly ladies that come and go, nudge or tug and then vanish.

In the fall of 2007, I received a call from Robert Dominguez, a feature writer and editor for *The New York Daily News*. Dominguez was doing a cover story for the *Daily News* Sunday Travel Section about ghost hunting in the tri-state area and decided Cape May might work for the piece. I decided to treat him to Cape May's original haunted house, the Emlen Physick Estate.

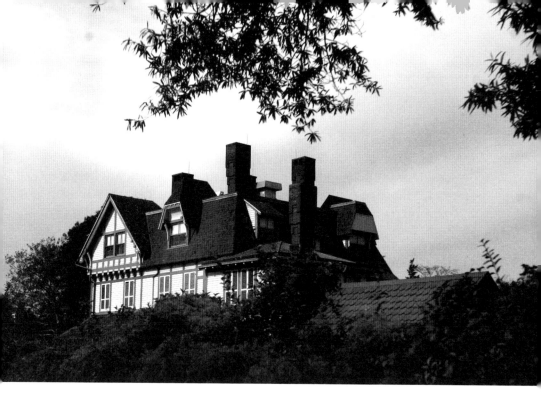

The Physick Estate is a living museum. With the exception of the original family and then a neighbor, the only other people that have occupied the mansion are employees of the Mid-Atlantic Center for the Arts (MAC) who today use the house as their base. The third floor houses offices for MAC, but the rest of the house is basically restored to the way it was in the Physicks time period. When a house remains unoccupied for so many years, the original tenants might not want to leave. For them it is like paradise: peaceful, quiet and basically eternity in Cape May. Except for daily tourists, the Physick family rarely shares their roost. This solemn setting can create one *great* haunting scenario!

I called down Gerry Eisenhaur, a friend from Boston who is a computer genius and great with all kinds of technical equipment. Gerry also happens to love ghost hunting and I thought the evening would benefit from his stable of ghost hunting equipment. My photographer

Maciek Nabrdalik was also in from Poland shooting for *Book 3* and I had him join us for the evening.

I felt like I was Ethel Mertz doing her "Madame Mertzola contacts the dead" routine from the *I Love Lucy* episode, "The Séance." There I was sat, around a small round table inside a big old dark house in front of Willy, two *Daily News* reporters, photographers, a technician and several members of MAC. They were all watching and waiting for me to perform. Let me tell you, there is no better way to lose concentration than to have a crowd of people staring at you while you try to contact the dead — and it wasn't just contacting the dead. That was the easy part. Getting them to actually put on a performance for these reporters was the challenge!

I lead the entire group, with their buzzing, humming equipment, flashing cameras and all, through the darkened hallways of the Physick mansion. We spent almost two hours in the old house. I had told the ghosts that a big New York reporter was in the house and asked if they could please give this lovely, yet somewhat skeptical gentleman a good dose of paranormal pudding. Nothing happened. No footsteps, no voices, not even one lousy cold spot. There were feelings around the house, but generally nothing paranormal was happening. Nothing. I had to pick the night the Physicks were out haunting someone else's home!

The only decent piece of evidence that Robert Dominguez received was a Class A EVP that said, "Speak for us." I told him I felt this meant the ghosts wanted him to tell their story. At the time he recorded the EVP, only he and Gerry were up on the second floor. I was too busy being disgusted, sitting with the rest of the group in the parlor on the first floor because nothing paranormal had happened. We finally get a big New York paper to come to Cape May, and the ghosts are gone. GONE.

That was in early October 2007, when I was also planning a new event with MAC called "Midnight at The Physick Estate." This would be basically the same idea as my *Daily News* tour except with 25 peo-

Technician Gerry Eisenhaur searches the ethers of the Physick hallway with the FLIR thermal imaging camera for signs of ghost movement.

ple instead of 11. The time would also be 11 PM until midnight, and it would take place on Halloween weekend.

As I prepared for Halloween week, a huge time in Cape May, the thought that the ghosts may still be inactive kept crossing my mind. Would the midnight tour be a paranormal dud as well? Had I brought too many people at once into the old mansion and scared the ghosts off? If 11 scared them away, 25 would keep them away for the week! Things were already set into motion, and I decided to move forward and put positive energy out to everyone involved that night.

As we gathered in the shadow of the great house, the damp, cold autumn air began to wrap around us. First our legs, then the rest of our bodies began to freeze slowly as I stood making some opening remarks about the house. The only thing keeping the tour-goers warm

at that point was some excess adrenaline running through their trembling bodies!

    The group moved into the Physick mansion and right away I felt this strange sense of comfort overwhelm me. I was anything but comfortable. I had been doing ghost tours for the last two days and had just completed three back-to-back trolley tours before rushing over to the Physick Estate for the 11 PM tour. I was, quite frankly, exhausted and fearful that the ghosts would let us down. You can never tell when a haunting will be active. Ghosts have their own schedules, and they don't make me privy to their plans!

    I first took the group up the stairs through the series of bedrooms. We stopped in Aunt Emilie's room first. This room has a billiard table (which I hope someday will be moved back up to the third floor where it belongs.) This is also the room where many people have reported feeling dizzy. Since Emilie is the key ghost in the house, I always feel this room should be more active. I suppose she never has time to relax, tending to other ghostly household matters. Tonight however, I felt several presences in the room with us. The room was packed with the living, but tonight cold spots were moving all around us — and the windows were *not* open. Next it was on to Mrs. Ralston's room.

Frances Ralston was the first to go. She died in 1915, followed the next year by her son, Dr. Emlen Physick. Her bedroom always has the darkest feel of any room in the house. Many people who are intuitive experience feelings of unease here. People on my tours reported feeling nauseous or getting a sudden headache or even feeling "pressure" around them while standing in this bedroom.

I don't think Frances Ralston is still in the house. Even though she was reported to run the house with an iron fist, I think this strong will would have sent her packing for Heaven upon her death. There is a combination of residual energy and actual spirit energy in that room. The residual energy is like a tape loop, playing repeatedly again feelings left over from Ralston's tenure at the house. The strong presence she used to have still dominates the psychic airwaves of her bedroom, but it is a repeat broadcast. She has not been home in years.

Isabelle, her younger sister who died in 1883 shortly after the family moved into the mansion, is probably the one hanging around with Emilie. Bella, as she was called by the family, was not well and probably stayed upstairs most of the time. I am not sure from what disease she succumbed, but the feeling of someone being ill pervades the ethers of that room.

The house has four main bedrooms on the second floor. One is Dr. Physick's library. This room was most likely Bella's bedroom for the first couple of years until she died. It would make sense that if there were four family members and four rooms on the second floor, they would all have been bedrooms in the early days. Since Bella's room is now Dr. Physick's library with the bedroom furniture removed, Bella may be occupying her sister's former bedroom. If indeed the ghosts see the way things are now, then Bella would realize her bedroom was gone and she had to sleep elsewhere.

Frances Ralston's bedroom is truly the paranormal hot spot in the house. The atmosphere makes people's skin crawl! As we stood in the room, something kept knocking. We looked around the room and noticed a shutter by the widow started banging and the stopped when we approached it. A lone shutter banging on a window was not anything paranormal to write home about. It is actually a common cause of what people "think" is a haunting, right up there with a loose window pain rattling in the night. This was different. The shutter was on the *inside* of the window and the window was closed! We checked for a draft and there was none. Something was moving the shutter back and forth. As I herded the group from the room a few last tour-goers called to me and pointed to the shutter across the room. It was at it again — opening and closing about three inches. Was someone trying to look out the window — or *into* the window?

Across the hall in Dr. Physick's library the group gathered to come up for air after the heaviness of Mrs. Ralston's bedroom. I suddenly sensed a man standing in the room — something I had never sensed before. Was this the ghost of Dr. Physick? Or another male presence paying a visit on the Physick family? A cold spot manifested and began to dart in and around the group. It seemed to come to a rest near a table in the center of the library. One of the tour-goers commented that she had just heard footsteps across the hallway in Mrs. Ralston's room. The library seemed to drop in temperature and various people began reporting cold spots. Cold spots can be a calling card of a ghost or ghosts, and everyone was pretty confident that *something* was in the room with us.

I attempted to contact the ghost to determine if it was indeed the ghost of Emlen Physick. Psychically, the energy appeared to be Physick's. Had he come back for a visit or was he hiding out at the house all this time? I could feel the energy move away without making any further contact. Each time we entered a room in the house, the ghostly occupants of that room moved somewhere else. This is likely the case with many hauntings. Ghosts may enjoy socializing with other ghosts, but they want to be left alone by humans. I guess the Physicks were no different that evening.

It was almost midnight, and I had promised the group a real authentic séance in the family parlor downstairs. We moved down the darkened main staircase into the foyer below and slowly assembled into the parlor next to the old pedal organ. We noticed one of the keys was down on the organ. A ghost symphony in progress? There's nothing like an old organ suddenly belting out a discordant tune (by itself) in the middle of a séance! Channeling ghosts with a small group can be difficult. Channeling ghosts with 25 living adults standing around watching is almost impossible—but I tried my best.

I allowed myself to relax, closed my eyes and tried to forget anyone else was in the room with me. I put myself in a slightly altered state of consciousness and sent out a psychic message to the entire house that I wanted/needed to make contact. Within minutes the house started to creak and settle. Then came the footsteps—first on the stairs coming down—then walking around above us in Mrs. Ralston's room. I knew no one else had been in the house prior to our arrival, because when we arrived the two guides from MAC had turned off the alarm system for the entire house so that we could enter.

Footsteps were heard above us. I asked the group to remain quiet as the house noises grew louder. A baby's cry was heard coming from the front bedroom! As far as I know there were no babies in the house in the Physick's time. A woman's voice was heard talking just out of range. Then there was what sounded like a dog barking. Dr. Physick had many furry friends, so that was not too strange — but a baby?

I could feel Emilie's energy moving around us. I asked her a few questions about the house. There were cold spots then more bumps and bangs upstairs. Suddenly a door closed in one of the bedrooms. My trance state may have stirred things up in the house, but did little to make a psychic connection between myself and the ghosts. I must admit my excitement kept me from focusing and staying in a trance state. I knew this was a rare and special moment in a ghost investigation, where things just start to happen and they can stop as quickly as they started. I disbanded the séance and asked people to move quietly into the hallway behind us. Once we were assembled, I stood on the stairs and told everyone to concentrate their senses. I found many of the group had some degree of intuitive or downright psychic ability. I was drawn to haunted houses and ghosts because of the pull from this ability; others apparently are drawn by the energies as well.

At that point, I glanced up to the stairway landing and noticed light coming from the doorway that lead to the servants' quarters. Everyone agreed that when we came down the stairs, that door was firmly closed. *Something* had reopened it while we were in the parlor.

I asked for a few volunteers, and we went through that very doorway and into the servants wing finding the door to the servant's bedroom was now also open! The wing was also *ice cold*. Not just drafty, but as cold as *death*. Someone was standing directly in our space and none of us was going to wait for a proper greeting. We left and closed the door behind us.

During my *Daily News* event, I had also felt someone was lurking in the servants' quarters. The name "Alice" kept repeating, and MAC

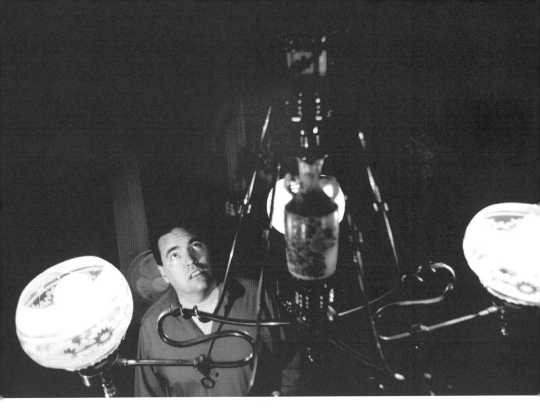

Craig listens to the ghostly voices and phantom footsteps coming from Mrs. Ralston's bedroom above.

Deputy Director Mary Stewart mentioned there once was an "Alice Johnson" who cooked for the Physicks. Could Aunt Emilie have kept her original cook?

It was now almost 1 AM, and I needed to wrap up the tour and get myself to bed. I thanked everyone and wished them all a Happy Halloween and proceeded to choral them to the front door. We were not five feet from the door when someone exclaimed, "Listen!"

Upstairs, two women could be heard laughing and talking to each other! The group rushed back into the hallway to listen. Next, a man's voice was heard, coming from another room upstairs! Each time we tried to leave the voices would start up, loud and clear. It was like they were baiting us to come back — and we did!

Those voice manifestations were some of the strongest and clearest haunting phenomena I had encountered in my career. Oh, I have heard something call my name, and an occasional laugh or two, but I had heard *nothing* like this. Was it the time of night or the combination of so many intuitives that brought out the sound track of the Physick Estate?

The *pièces de résistance* of the evening came last. One of the guys on the tour had been standing at the bottom of the stairway and exclaimed, "Hey check it out—somebody's playing an old Victrola upstairs!"

The sounds of a scratchy old record playing wafted down the grand staircase, which sent shivers down the spines of everyone. Most of us could hear the music, which we thought was really cool. However, the finishing touch was when one of the guides from MAC exclaimed to the people on the other end of the group by the front door, "But we don't have a Victrola! Or anything that plays music upstairs!"

How cool was that? Victrola music, but no Victrola in the house—at least not now.

I asked for two brave volunteers to ascend the dark staircase and place themselves firmly in the middle of the pitch black hallway, on the second floor, in the center of the paranormal storm. Would you have done it?

Two young ladies leaped to position and when they were in place I told them I would ask the ghosts to make contact with them. Within seconds of my request more footsteps could be heard, and I psychically could feel two presences moving toward them. There was a brief shriek, but the two volunteers held their own against the ghosts. Both ladies reported feeling something go "right through them" twice. Like cold, tingly energy. The ghosts moved past them and must have gone through the servants hallway because they did not come downstairs.

The volunteers returned to the group. Our goal had been achieved: make contact with the spirit world at the Physick Estate. We now had made both mental and physical contact.

As we all moved to the open front doorway, a huge burst of cold air pushed at our backs from the stairway. Were the Physicks saying goodbye? Or were they just trying to get rid of us so they could have some piece and quiet in the house? I don't think our group would ever see the paranormal in the same light again. If there were skeptics at the start of the tour, they had now probably changed sides!

As we said goodnight to the guides, I glanced up at the outside of the building. I could have sworn that something moved the curtain in a second floor window. The guides activated the motion detectors and alarm. I was now convinced no one was hiding up on the third floor playing games on us. If anyone was there, the alarm would have been tripped.

Driving away from the Physick Estate on that moonlit night in October, I kept thinking to myself what ghosts must do to keep themselves occupied for hundreds of years. Did our "Midnight at the Physick Estate" amuse them? Perhaps for fun they run a "Morning at the Physick Estate" tour showing their other ghostly friends what it is like to live in a house overrun with the living! Do they see us? Can they hear us? Are we the ghosts to them?

If you should happen to visit the Physick Estate on the right evening — you might just get the answer to some of those questions!

Cape May's original haunted house never disappoints. Aunt Emilie and the crew outdid themselves that evening. It was one of the best haunting experiences I have had in my career. Hopefully she will treat us to a few repeat performances in the future!

There are very few *real* haunted mansions of this caliber that are open to the public. If you love the paranormal, this house is a must visit! For more info, visit MAC's website *www.capemaymac.org*.

The Parris Cottage
JONAS MILLER RETURNS — FROM THE DEAD
Private Cottage - 204 Perry Street

THOSE who know me well will know where to find me at night in Cape May. If I am not chasing disembodied spirits around dark hallways in town, I am probably enjoying the other kind of spirits at one of my favorite haunts, The Virginia Hotel. Between the fabulous Ebbitt Room Restaurant and the charming cocktail lounge — and of course, its location on haunted Jackson Street — The Virginia is a great place to kick back and relax before an evening of ghost hunting.

Throughout the years, many wonderful bartenders have worked at the Virginia. One of the more recent keepers of the spirits was Gina Melcher. One night while I was chatting with Gina about ghosts and hauntings, and she mentioned she and her boyfriend had some interesting experiences at his family home right up the street. The house, as it turned out, was one of the original homes in town with the oldest section dating back to the 1830s. However, the most interesting historical fact about this property was who had built it — none other than Jonas Miller, the current ghost patriarch of Congress Hall!

It always amazes me when a historical property like this one sits unnoticed for so many years. The house was called The Parris Inn or The Parris Cottage for as long as anyone can remember. Why this was not called The Miller Cottage, I do not know. Maybe Jonas Miller felt Congress Hall was his baby, and the little cottage on Perry Street was just a temporary home. For whatever reason, this venerable old cottage has stood quietly on Perry Street for almost 200 years without anyone even noticing. It is also one of the oldest haunts in town.

Speaking at length to Gina about the cottage in which she and her boyfriend Mike Haggerty lived, reminded me that a lot of people who have grown up in town, have also grown up with ghosts. Many people might never admit it, but if you grew up in an old home in Cape May, the chances you were cohabiting with a ghost or two were pretty high. In April of 2007, I finally made a date to meet Gina and Mike at their home. I gathered up our gear, my partner Willy, our tech specialist Gerry Eisenhaur and his future wife Erin Long, and we walked over to the Parris, ready to ghost hunt.

The Parris Inn had been run for many years by Mike's parents as a rooming house. The house was a throwback to Cape May's days prior to the B&Bs and fancy hotels. In those days the guests would make do with a room with a small kitchenette and bathroom while spending a week or two at the shore. Mike continued renting out rooms to many old customers who enjoyed the convenient location to the beach and prices that were a downright bargain.

Very little of the house had changed over the years. Mike's Dad and later Mike himself continued to upgrade the rooms, but it was evident that the old homestead needed a complete face lift to catch up with the times and needs of today's shore visitors.

Entering the old home, I felt multiple ghosts roaming around the building. The house was composed of a dizzying array of rooms and hallways that went up three stories. Below the house was hand-dug basement with a labyrinth of passageways. The interior energy of this house featured a bleed through between layers of time. Standing in some of the rooms completely threw off my psychic balance. If I had not occasionally gazed out the window, I could well have been standing in another century! The house had layers of residual energy floating around, and I was floating right along with it!

Mike took us on a tour of the house, room by room. As we made our way through the older part of the house, Gerry started to set up a camera and noticed he was bleeding. Somehow he scratched himself. We noted it and moved into the back, older section of the house.

Gina first told us her encounter at the house back at The Virginia. She awoke one night and saw a strange orange cloud of energy at the foot of the bed. It was late at night and by the time she woke Mike it had vanished. Mike added that his mother had experienced the same orange energy in a small bedroom in the oldest section of the house. Energy may have color sometimes, but I have never heard of ghost's energy described as "orange." Blue, white, green even yellow, but orange was a first!

We entered the small bedroom in the oldest section of the house. It had been used for storage for a number of years and looked like a run-down Victorian furnished room where one would expect to find Oscar Wilde on his deathbed! It was a mess, but it had *great* atmosphere.

"There is a staircase missing," I told Gina and Mike. "It was in here and I can sense a woman walking up and down."

"Wow!" Gina exclaimed looking to Mike.

"You're right, there was, there was — 'cause there is another set of stairs right above us and there was a set of stairs in here — but those stairs have been gone since before I was born," Mike recalled.

The woman I sensed still followed her old pathways in the house. The ghosts could still see and use the original servants' stairway, even though it was long gone. It is experiences like this one that lend credibility to the "bleed-through of time" theory. A ghost is a field of energy with a consciousness. It could theoretically pass through a solid wall as some waves of energy can pass through solid matter. Was I seeing a residual image from years ago? Or was I viewing through time and space to the early days of the house when the staircase existed? Time is not linear. It may be possible to jump psychically between time periods while remaining in the same physical location. It would kind of suck if ghosts turned out to be nothing more than people from other times bleeding through to our time. The fact that they are dead makes them much more interesting, I think!

I was picking up imagery of someone cooking on a large iron stove, and Mike validated that information. The room was once a kitchen. The name "Bonnie" kept flashing into my head. Was Bonnie a former

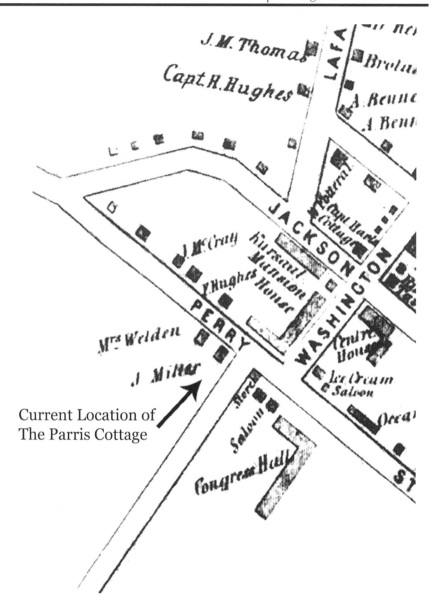

Inset of Numan's 1850 Map of "Cape Island" showing the earlier version of Congress Hall and Jonas Miller's Cottage behind on Perry Street.

servant? She appeared to me as tall and slender with a long neck and wearing a long flowing dress. Someone from Jonas Miller's time?

According to Mike Haggerty, Jonas Miller built the house between 1835 and 1840 on part of a 60-acre tract that was called "The Congress Hall Plantation." In those days, Congress Hall sat further back from the ocean. There were several other buildings on the property, including Miller's cottage.

We moved between a few of the first rooms until we stopped in one of the bedrooms, where I attempted to contact the "lady of the house." Gina said she felt the presence she encountered was a woman. Mike was not sure if the ghost that he felt "sitting on his chest" in the middle of one night was a man or a woman.

Gerry commented that the room temperature had begun to drop. First by two degrees and then by two more. I sensed something out in the hallway. Gerry's fiancée Erin reported feeling something in her vicinity by the doorway. The room got colder and colder and everyone was feeling it. Someone had joined us. I was also getting a name like "Louisa" as this was all happening. Was this another one of Miller's staff or perhaps a family member? This is assuming, of course, that these were ghosts from his lifetime. Jonas Miller died in 1869 in Camden, New Jersey and may have sold the house by that time or lived elsewhere in town.

Mike pulled out a history of the house he had in his desk. He could not find anyone named "Bonnie," but he did find a "Louisa Mount." Louisa Mount had owned the house only a short time, from 1897 until her death in 1905. I suppose anyone who owned the house could be haunting it, even if they only were living there for eight years. Right after Mike confirmed that Louisa was one of the owners, something knocked the tape recorder from my hand! I picked the hand-held cassette recorder up off the floor, put it back together and turned it on. I suddenly found that I had two red scratches on the back of my hand. Had something scratched my hand and I then unconsciously jerked my hand away?

Opposite: Family Portrait of Jonas Miller (1785-1869)

38 The Parris Cottage

Perry Street 1908. Not much has changed in Cape May in 100 years. The Parris Cottage is on the far left. (Courtesy of Walt Campbell)

    I noticed Erin was very sensitive to the ghostly energy of the house. At this point, she started to become nauseous and needed to sit out in the fresh air on the from porch. I have seen this happen to others on investigations. If you do not keep yourself grounded and focused, you will suck up all of the residual energy like a sponge. This feeling is the same as eating too much food too quickly. Luckily, with my ADD, my mind tends to drop most of the feelings it picks up, so I will not become overloaded with residual thoughts and energies. I also need to run a tape recorder so I actually can recall what happened on each investigation! I felt the ghostly woman was circling around Erin, almost as if she recognized her from some other time or place.

    The ghosts were having a field day playing with the room temperature. It was warm, then it was freezing, and vice versa. Mike was not reacting like this was a normal occurrence of the house as he too was feeling the rapid change in temperature. I felt a ghost circling around us. The ghost was very curious that we were interested in the history of the house and specifically—which previous owners might be doing the haunting. I began to wonder if anyone else over the years had ever bothered to investigate the ghosts on this property.

At this point in the investigation, Gerry, Erin and I were distracted by someone walking around upstairs in the hallway and in the room above us. I thought Gina had gone upstairs, but when she appeared from the downstairs bathroom and the footsteps continued above, I knew we were hearing something paranormal. The temperature continued to drop. It was getting colder in the room.

"Who's upstairs in the room above us?" I asked Mike.

"No one else is in the house—do you hear something up there?"

We all agreed something was up there, and I ascended the staircase to find out.

The entire house had a feeling of being out of time, like it was sitting in some kind of time warp. Once I made it to the top of the first staircase, I felt as if I had just climbed Mount Everest! My senses were off and I was more in a dream state than an awake state. The ghosts were much closer to me now—I wondered if they knew I was there.

There was an incredible feeling of heaviness to the upstairs hallway. It was a dense sensation like something was all around us. The first bedroom I entered was definitely "live." It had such a strong energy, I was not sure that I could stay in the room more than a few moments. This type of feeling overwhelms the intuitive both physically and mentally. I walked right in on a ghost rocking in the chair!

A different ghost sat in the rocker in this bedroom on the second floor. The group moved in and Gerry took some ambient readings. I started to get the name "Will" which soon turned into "Willis." Mike confirmed a woman with that last name had owned the house at one point. The energy was getting stronger, and we all started to get chills. The hair began to stand up on my arms and neck. One theory for this is that ghosts exist as a field of negatively charged ions, and when we encounter that negative field we feel a cold sensation and the hair on our arms and neck will tend to stand up. It is similar to the sensation generated by one of those ionic air purifiers. The air is charged with negative ions and feels cool and moist.

Had I made a direct hit with the name Willis? Did the ghost in the room happen to be a Willis or be related to someone with that name? Something was making the energy spike. I reassured the group that the energy we were experiencing was *not* negative. It was strong, but benevolent.

Gerry noticed the floors on the second level were all covered with carpet. When we heard the footsteps from below, it sounded like people walking on uncarpeted, hardwood floors. How was this possible? Were we hearing ghostly footsteps walking on the original floors? Do ghosts only interact with physical things from their own time?

We moved down the hallway to a back bedroom where both Mike and Gina had felt presences. Once everyone got into the room I quieted the group down and asked the ghosts for a physical sign that they were near. I had the tape recorder running.

Later, when I reviewed the tape, in the background noise you can hear an EVP of a man saying, "Did you hear that?"

After which a second voice replies, "What?"

This is followed by a woman responding something like, "They are channelable," which was a word I had never heard used before. Were the ghosts hearing us in some diminished capacity? There is always this nagging question as to just how they hear or see us. It's like they are in a room on the other side of a wall from us and if we put our ear to the wall we can hear them and vice versa. Otherwise we do not even notice each other.

I asked the ghosts if they were walking around on the second floor. An EVP appears on the tape following my question with a man saying, "we've got your ball" or "pickup your ball." This is one of problems with EVPs. Many times EVPs make no sense in context to the question being asked by the living questioner. This makes me think that once again, I was recording ghosts having a conversation with themselves that had nothing to do with us. If a man was telling someone to "pickup your ball," maybe he was addressing a ghostly child?

After that, the room got quiet and even the EVPs stopped on the tape. Nothing but white noise. The ghostly voices were gone from the recording from that point forward. Gerry reported the EMF readings dropped back to normal. It had been up around 1.2 with the normal readings between zero and 0.5. Erin checked the air temperature with the digital thermometer, and while the readings continued to fluctuate. It started to feel warmer to all of us in the room. The ghosts kept moving and going about their business. Other than the circling ghost on the first floor, no other ghost seemed to notice our presence. Mike made a comment that the rooms in the house just go on and on and we decided to continue our tour before I became too drained. There is only a certain amount of energy in my psychic batteries and I needed to save some of that energy in case we encountered anything else in the house that might tip the paranormal scale.

Like many houses this old, there have been structural renovations done to Jonas Miller's original cottage over the years. Mike told me there was a "100 year renovation" done when the original L-shaped house was first modernized, followed by a 1970s renovation done by his father when a new wing was added on in back. Jonas Miller would hardly recognize his old homestead today.

The house was a maze of rooms and hallways—three floors and a cottage worth. The energy in here was all over the place and I kept trying to refocus myself psychically for each room. This was the Thanksgiving dinner of ghost investigations—and I was starting to get that "too much intake, too fast" feeling.

Writing about one ghost who does the same routine in one small house is so much easier than writing about multiple ghosts. Because a ghost comes and goes so quickly, one never knows for sure if it is the same ghost or another persona all together. This house was like being on a ride in an amusement park—twisting and turning in some little two seater car along a track weaving through dark hallways. One minute something is jumping out at you, the next it is quiet and dark and then it starts all over again. I kept thinking a vacation in a calm, non-haunted resort would be nice.

We climbed yet another staircase and made our way to the attic. Mike told us the third floor was the attic of the original house. It had several bedrooms and as we passed one particular room we all got a bad feeling.

"This room has weird energy," I told the group, hesitating to enter but prodding Erin to be the guinea pig for the group and go inside.

"I never liked that room," Gina told us, "I just don't like going in there."

Mike agreed that he used to enjoy sleeping in another room across the hallway as a child, but that one room he found "uncomfortable." Even to work in there made him uneasy. What is it about a room like this that gives many people the same "stay away" feeling?

I think it is a type of territorial energy that radiates from a ghost's mind, similar to psychic energy a living person or animal will give off when they do not want to be bothered. It was not an evil energy in this room, just a "back off" energy.

There was an EVP on the tape that either said, "Hit the road," or "Hit the door." It was a man's voice, and it was possibly the presence we were feeling inside the room. The cassette tape ended as I moved into the room, and by the time we reloaded a new cassette the group was heading down yet another set of stairs to the second floor.

As we moved down Gerry felt the door to the "occupied" bedroom may have closed about three inches. There were automatic door closers on all of the doors, so that might have somehow been triggered by our walking by.

We walked across the second floor again, a man named "George" arrived. He was not a ghost. Instead he was a spirit coming back from the Other Side with messages for Mike. Mike confirmed his Dad was George and he had passed in 1996. His Dad wanted to give him some various points of advice about the house. I felt Mike was very attached to the house, but had trouble maintaining all that needed to be done and his Dad was there to help. I was informed only much later that the house was being sold, and Mike would soon be turning over the old place to a new owner.

George Haggerty's spirit tried to reassure Gina that she should not be afraid of the ghosts in the house. He told them, "They are all guests living or dead. When you run a hotel, you have to take in all types, you can't turn away business." The group had a good laugh. George also kept making these odd "popping noises" and Mike laughed and confirmed his dad used to make noises like that.

It was apparent that Mike loved the house and his Dad knew that. Mike had said he would love to see the old house restored. We had a wonderful exchange between father and son for the next 30 minutes or so. The bond was strong and his Dad wanted to make sure Mike knew he was there to help. George's energy completely swept out any remaining ghostly energy. The ghosts must have recognized their former innkeeper and were giving him space.

Since Mike's Dad had come through, the ghosts seemed to take a back seat. George was a very strong presence in the house. When spirits come back from heaven, do they see and interact with the ghosts? There is a dynamic to this equation that we do not yet understand and perhaps we will only come to realize after we too have died. Are ghosts and spirits more closely related than I once thought? Are the

ghosts simply vacationing spirits back visiting for a while?

After the channeling, we decided to have a look at the "catacombs" in the cellar. Mike's Dad had spent years digging out tunnels in the old cellar so that he could move around under the house when things needed to be repaired. The cellar, like the house above it, was sprawling. I felt like I was on some archeological dig. Mike showed us the remnants of an old well in the cellar. Later showed us his collection of bottles found during another one of his "digs" in the back yard. The catacombs were clear of ghostly activity.

We emerged from the catacombs dusty, but ghost-free. Since the tunnels were only dug by George Haggerty, in the 1960s and 1970s, the ghosts would no business there, since was only dirt and no cellar in their time. A house this old also may have ghosts spanning several generations.

As we walked past the old mirror in the hallway of the house, as we were leaving the Parris Inn, that day back in April of 2007. For just a split second, I thought I caught a glimpse of a woman standing and watching us. Then she vanished as quickly as she had appeared. Mirrors can play tricks on us, but then again, so can ghosts.

A 175-year-old house like this can also have newly made ghosts of people who have died more recently. Here is a house that has changed very little over the centuries. The building is a mix of building styles from many different eras. There is a ghostly mix as well.

There are at present three ghosts haunting the Parris Cottage. Two women and one man. The women's names for now, are Bonnie and Louisa. The man is still unidentified. There may also be a boy present. I felt fortunate that I had the chance to get into the house while it was still in its former state. Hopefully, someday, renovations will be down and the Miller Cottage will shine once again.

An old house like the Parris Cottage certainly holds a lot of cards close to the paranormal vest. The answers are all there, but we are not privy to them, at least not while we are alive.

In late 2007, Mike Haggerty and his brother sold the Parris Cottage to the owners of Congress Hall. I felt this was a fitting reunion of properties for old Cape May. At present the hotel is using the house for staff's quarters. I hope that one day they may restore it and once again rename it "Miller Cottage." The Parris Cottage or Inn was the name given to the house about 1900, when it began its life as a boarding house. Historically, the house should be called "The Jonas Miller Cottage."

On one of my later visits, the ghosts mentioned that Miller would be returning to his old roost. Since he is presently haunting Congress Hall, it will not be a long walk, not even for a ghost. Somehow it just feels right that the properties are joined again. In Cape May, things change all the time, but eventually everything goes back to its historical roots. Welcome home, Jonas — after almost 200 years of running Congress Hall, you deserve some R & R!

The Bacchus Inn

WINE — AND SPIRITS

B&B 710 Columbia Avenue

MY first foray into the paranormal on this end of Columbia Avenue was at this B&B, at the time of my visit called The Inn at Journey's End. I had met the new owners of the Inn on one of Diane Bixler's Haunted Cape May walking tours. Diane had just added the house to her tour, and she was anxious to have me meet the owners. I returned a few nights later on a dark and stormy summer evening and conducted a séance in the dining room of the house.

The house had started out as a private residence, thought to have been built around 1872 by local builder Enos Williams. Over the years, the rooms were turned into apartment units and finally the house was converted into a B&B. My first impression of the house was how much energy there was cooped up in the space. While I had been doing channeling for some time, psychically reading houses was not my forté and, back in those days, I was still a little green at the practice. This was one of my first encounters with multi-layered energies. I thought the best thing I could do was contact the strongest ghost first and then work my way through the crowd.

"I am getting a name like Conwell," I told the owners at the time. At first, I thought I may have just been picking up the name from across the street. At the time, Corbin and Linda Cogswell owned the Linda Lee. One of the proprietors said there was a "Fanny Conwell" on the list of deed holders; she had owned the house in the 1930s and 1940s. I felt good about hitting the nail on the head the first time and focused on the name Fanny Conwell.

The ghostly woman appeared to me to be in her late fifties or early sixties. She was fussing about something in the bathroom off the downstairs common area. I did not want to be too prying, as you never know just what old habits a ghost may be hanging on to... and she was in the bathroom!

I focused on Fanny Conwell and tried to put out a psychic line announcing who I was and that I would like to speak with her. She did not respond. What she did come back with was very strange. She was muttering about a roast not cooking properly. I could then see her leaning over and poking at something. I think it was a stove. What was stove—not to mention a roast—doing in her *bathroom?*

In a few moments, the mystery was solved. One of the current proprietors of the house told me that when he was renovating downstairs he had discovered that what is now the bathroom was at one time a kitchen. Now we were cooking with gas!

48   The Bacchus Inn

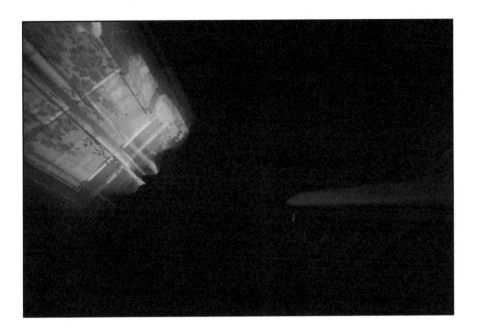

Fanny would not give me the time of day. It was one complaint after another about that stupid roast. She would not respond to any of my questions, and I started to wonder if she were only a residual haunting. Residual hauntings, to refresh from the previous books, are tape loops. They are trapped energies that play out in the form of mental images to those who are sensitive. Sometimes these images happen so fast they take on the appearance of a ghost. The difference is that a ghost's actions are constantly changing, and a ghost might interact with the living, whereas a residual haunting is static and does not interact. The same event appears to happen repeatedly. Was Fanny Conwell a residual energy? She certainly was complaining loud enough. I felt like marching into that kitchen/bathroom and telling her, "No wonder your roast doesn't taste right — you've been cooking it for 70 years!" I decided instead to move on to the next ghost.

It was about this point in the channeling that I sensed a young boy moving around the outside of the house. Several people had reported seeing a young boy darting in and out of the alleyway between the houses on that part of Columbia Avenue. As I channeled that evening the spirit of a boy calling himself "Brendan" came through. He would not come into the house as he had been told by his previous employers never to enter the upstairs of a home. From what I could tell, Brendan had worked in some capacity delivering coal. He also mentioned a passing horse cart had injured his legs, and he walked with crutches. Unlike Fanny Conwell, this ghost was very interactive.

When we rented a house nearby on Columbia Avenue last summer, Stephanie Kirk from The Linda Lee and The Bedford had told me that when they gutted that house, a child's wheelchair from the Victorian era had been discarded on the trash. I wondered if Brendan had possibly lived in this other house during his lifetime in Cape May. I write more about Brendan in the *Paranormal Playground* chapter in *Book 2*. One thing I have found in the investigations in this book is the preponderance of children's ghosts in town. They seem to be everywhere.

After finishing the channeling that evening I conducted a walk-through of the house. On the second floor, sitting on an old fainting couch by the window, I encountered the ghost of an older woman in her 80s. She turned and smiled at me, and then turned back to gaze out the window. She had a wonderful, soft, mellow energy and just seemed at peace with where she was. She gave me the feeling that she was waiting for someone to come down the road. She never said anything more.

One of the more common haunting signs in the old house at 710 Columbia was footsteps going up to the third floor. Many people reported hearing the noises, but nothing was ever found when the area was checked. Why do ghosts create footsteps? I ask myself this question many times. Phantom footsteps are the most common of all haunting phenomena and manifest in most haunted places at one time or another.

My theory is that since ghosts are thought to be fields of energy, that energy can interact with the physical on our plane of existence. We sometimes feel cold spots move in and around us that we associate with ghosts. If this is representative of a ghost's energy, then that energy has a physical feel to it. Is this energy focused to reflect the shape of a physical body and can this "energy body" affect matter around it? I think in some way it can and does. Cold spots are a calling card of a ghost. If we can feel a ghost's body as "cold", we are physically interacting with it.

Some people have reported being touched by a ghost or pushed or pinched. In order for a ghost to do this, they have to get physical. Ghosts must have the ability to "turn on" a physical body or to enter into a state where their energy is nearer to our energy and these physical exchanges can take place more easily. I don't think that ghosts deliberately try to create sounds of footsteps. I think it is more likely they have entered into this closer state of being and their energy is colliding with our energy by default. The most common haunting phenomenon at 710 Columbia, now called The Bacchus seems to be these phantom footsteps.

On one stay with the previous owners a few years back, I happened to awake in the middle of the night to see my ceiling fan had turned itself back on. The shadowy blades of the fan kept spinning around over my head. I grabbed my flashlight and shined the light to reveal what I had thought were fan blades—were in fact two bats flying around over my head! The previous owners had been doing some plumbing work in the ceiling and had left a small hole open to the outside. The charming winged rodents had decided to pay me a visit! I love animals, but not bats in my bedroom at 3 AM. I crawled out of the room under the safety of my comforter and lay out in the hallway on the second floor until morning. All throughout the night, I could hear footsteps on the stairs leading to the third floor. Something kept going up, but never came back down. Real ghosts or residual energy?

One of my favorite rooms at 710 Columbia was the bedroom that stuck out of the east side of the house. It was a light and airy room with lovely stained glass windows. Today, owners John and Lisa Matusiak

"Mrs. Mason's Room" on the second floor of the Bacchus Inn

have created a suite in that part of the house, incorporating that same room. During the tenure of the previous owners, I had stayed in that room quite a bit, and had encountered the ghost of a woman calling herself "Mrs. Mason," on several occasions. Mrs. Mason had apparently lived somewhere near Jackson Street and had been "put out" by the Great Fire. It was true that the fire never touched this part of town on Columbia Avenue way back in 1878. Just how long was Mrs. Mason planning on renting that room? The ghosts seemed to treat 710 Columbia as a boarding house, even after all of these years.

If ghosts are trying to get away from us and they enjoy spending time in Cape May, it must be a constant challenge to find a room in town without any annoying living people occupying it. Maybe the ghosts just vacation here in the winter!

The Bacchus Inn

Ghostly footsteps have been heard ascending the stairs to the third floor.

I spent many visits to Cape May staying at former Inn at Journey's End at 710 Columbia. Some of my fondest ghost experiences in town were in that old house. Since John and Lisa bought the property a few years ago, I had not gone back to stay there in quite some time. I had other houses to investigate (including their main house across the street,) and I had basically found all there was to find in the ethers at 710 Columbia. I did return to stay here once in 2007, and about the only experience I had was to hear the footsteps on the stairs during the night.

Lisa told me about a "ghost experience" John had at 710 one day recently. They now live with their son J. T. in the owner's quarters in the back of the house. One day while John was working in back he started hearing footsteps upstairs and on the back porch. As Lisa told me this story, I perked right up with excitement that they had finally experienced their ghosts!

"It was raccoons," Lisa finished with a smile, ending the story. Great, just what I needed to hear, another mammal story. It couldn't have even been *ghost* raccoons; it had to be the living kind!

I conducted some of my best early séances at 710 Columbia back in the 1990s. Something would always show up at the doors or through the walls of that house. The house always had a great feel, and I think the ghosts felt comfortable there as well. The real party crasher of those days was a ghost named Walter. It seemed the séance candles had barely burned for a minute when he would fly into the room like a moth to a flame.

When I go into a trance channeling state, my energy radiates from that spot and does create somewhat of a moth-flame effect. Trying to contact the ghosts in one house can be very difficult when trance channeling. In most cases, the longer I channel the wider my energy waves disperse, and ghosts from the street start migrating in my direction. This has happened up and down Columbia Avenue when I have trance channeled and, if I am not careful, I can be easily overwhelmed by an influx of ghost energies.

Walter was not as overwhelming as he was annoying. He seemed to be there just for himself, and he would not let me concentrate when he was present. He did not belong to 710 Columbia, but rather "lived" across the street at The Linda Lee. Ghosts have been known to seek me out; luckily, it doesn't happen that often!

Let's take a quick trip across the street to the Linda Lee and hear Walter's story.

The Linda Lee

THE CONNOISSEUR GHOST
AND HIS METAPHYSICAL MAID

B&B 725 Columbia Avenue

"MY name is Walter... I am from the Linda Lee and have come looking for some decent wine and cheese."

I remember the night well—late one summer evening, I was channeling for the proprietress of the B&B at 710 Columbia, that is now called The Bacchus. I was conversing with them and their ghosts when through the front wall of the house burst a larger than life spirit who identified himself as "Walter." It was not the first time this wandering sociable ghost had made his presence known outside of his abode—nor would it be the last.

At one point friends of mine asked the former owners of the Linda Lee about their "ghost" and about all they could recall of ghostly activity were a few phantom footsteps on the stairs. But here Walter was, and he was not leaving until he found some good libations.

Each time I attempted to channel 710 Columbia, this pesky ghost from 725 would move into our space announcing his arrival and inviting us to a wine and cheese party—that we were expected to furnish on his behalf. A ghost's life?

Spending almost 30 years of my life in the retail wine business, I could imagine myself doing the same when I cross over, should I happen to make a stop in Cape May on the way. Walter had an agenda, and if we were not pouring and slicing, we were not part of it.

I never really got to know Walter that well. Each time he would show his ghostly face, my friend who owned the B&B at the time would chastise him for ruining our local séance and shoo him away. Walter would usually oblige and we moved ahead to other ghostly goings on.

The Linda Lee

Years later, we were staying next door to The Linda Lee, at what was then called The Brass Bed, and is now part of The Bacchus Inn B&B group. Owner John Matusiak and I were discussing various haunts on the street and I mentioned Walter. He told me that he and his wife Lisa had good friends, Archie and Stephanie Kirk, who now owned The Linda Lee. The Kirks had also recently purchased The Bedford B&B on Stockton Street. John cautioned me not to say anything about ghosts to Stephanie because she was not comfortable talking about such things. Too bad I thought, I would love to get into the Linda Lee and psychically nose around, but there were other ghosts to gather in my writing and I moved on.

Curiosity eventually got the best of me. I told my partner Willy that we needed to stay at The Bedford the next time we came down. Since my early days at the neighboring Sea Holly Inn, I had heard stories of ghostly footsteps in The Bedford and I had never stayed there before. Cape May has so many wonderful B&Bs and inns that part of the fun of coming to town is to stay at a different place each time. The Bedford was due for a visit, even if there were no ghosts, at least none that I could talk about in front of Stephanie.

I decided not to unnerve the Kirks by telling them who I was. Most people in town knew me as "The Ghost Writer," but I was pretty sure I could stay incognito. I am very sensitive to other people's feelings on the subject of ghosts and hauntings and, if I sense someone becoming uncomfortable, I will not broach the subject.

The first afternoon at The Bedford, Archie Kirk, the B&Bs quintessential host, greeted us at the door. Stephanie smiled from the hallway and welcomed us from afar. John's previous warning, "Stephanie will freak out of you tell her she has ghosts," kept flashing through my mind, and I made a point of avoiding direct contact when we arrived.

One thing lead to another. We sat down for tea. Archie got called to the phone and Willy went up to the room to use the bathroom. There we were, me on the couch and Stephanie in the chair across from me by the fireplace, both of us nervously trying to be polite and make conversation. Had someone told her who I was?

Before the thought left my head, she calmly said, "So, what is this channeling thing you do?"

I thought I would choke on my cup of tea. Someone spilled the beans. Thanks, John.

Stephanie, as it turned out, was a very caring and open individual who respected other people's opinions while keeping her own. She and Archie were in fact two of the warmest, most down-to-earth individuals we had yet to meet in Cape May, and we have since become good friends.

Stephanie had been briefed about who I was and the ghost writing I did for *Exit Zero* newspaper and my books. The pressure to be incognito was off and we relaxed and had a great weekend at the seaside. At some point during that first stay at The Bedford, Stephanie asked if we wanted to see The Linda Lee. The Kirks had started out with the Linda Lee, but now resided at The Bedford, hiring an innkeeper at the time to run The Linda Lee for them.

The Linda Lee is really a throwback in time. Beautifully decorated with all the Victorian trimmings. I can remember the night we first sat around The Linda Lee's dining room table and Stephanie casually asked me, "The Bedford isn't haunted is it?"

"Not that I know of, but this house is and the ghost's name is Walter and he loves good wine and cheese," I told her.

There was a pause of silence which was soon broken by Archie putting his head in his hands and moaning, "Oh boy."

Stephanie looked pointedly at Archie to get the dirt. "Was there a Walter in this house, Arch?" she asked.

Archie gestured that he felt sure that he had seen a Walter in the listing of previous owners and went into the office and grabbed a folder that contained a comprehensive report done by historian Mike Conley of House Tales. House Tales will research the complete history of a home for its owners for a fee. Conley's work was quite thorough and included old newspaper articles, deed listings, names and dates of all the previous owners, *including a man named Walter.* You could have heard a pin drop in the room. I had found Walter, a few years late, but I had my ghost. At the time, I had just finished The Ghosts of Cape May *Book 2* and after Stephanie exclaimed to Walter to "move on to Heaven," I felt it best that Walter and his wine and cheese seance would have to wait for *Book 3*. Walter was dead then, he would still be dead in another year or two.

After getting to know Archie and Stephanie Kirk a little better, I decided it was time to pay an overnight visit to The Linda Lee. Stephanie told me that a few guests had told her they had some kind of experience in Felicia's Room at the top of the stairs on the second floor. People had reported seeing someone at the foot of the bed during the night. One interesting aspect of this room is an ancient, narrow spiral staircase that winds its way to the back part of the attic. Could a former servant be using the original staircase that he or she used back when? Ghosts will follow old paths.

The Linda Lee was closed for the month of January, but Archie agreed to let us spend the weekend to do our investigation. We set up base in the back of the house in Debbie's Room. On that first night, January 21, 2007, I waited until about 11 PM when all was quiet on the street and sat down in the parlor downstairs and started a recording session. After we returned home, I somehow misplaced the tape and never uploaded it onto my computer. Only now, in February of 2008 as I write this chapter, did I finally preview the tape. I am definitely the "ADD Medium." Stuff just takes forever to get done. Luckily I am working with people who are already dead.

This particular recording session proved quite interesting. When the hiss was removed from the recording, a myriad of ghostly voices was heard in the background noise of the tape. From the sound of this tape, one would think it was a summer night in July and I had the windows open to the noisy street. But, it was the dead of winter, when the dead of Cape May are the only ones moving (or talking) late at night in the B&Bs.

I seem to get a plethora of EVPs in some places. My friends, who are also into various areas of the metaphysical, have a theory that my mediumistic ability amplifies the number and quality of EVPs. Others tend to get one or two EVPs during an investigation, I have recorded dozens of EVPs at a time. I don't know why it happens, it just happens. The Linda Lee turned out to be one of those bonus tapes.

At times it sounded like two women conversing and other times a man and a child were talking. The responses to my questions came fast and in many cases were undecipherable. At least they were responding. That was a good thing.

I sat and meditated to try to connect with the spirits of the house, except the spirits were already there and they were *very* busy. I first asked if there was anyone there in the room with me.

The response was two female voices talking, the first says, "Did anyone vacuum in here?"

"I did," was the second, rather distorted sounding response.

Vacuum — hmmm — they're *vacuuming?* But what are they vacuuming? Do they have their own set of carpets on the Other Side? And what do they use to vacuum — a Boover? Obviously they had their own agenda, and I was not part of it at the moment.

A few more minutes into the tape I asked, "Is Walter here?"

"Walter is not in," was the response on the tape in a deep male voice. I asked the same question about fifteen minutes later and the voice snapped back, "I told you he's *not* in!" This is one problem with EVP recording; the ghosts can hear us, but we can only hear them when we play back the recording. In this case, it took me a year to play back the recording. Luckily the ghosts did not know that.

There were several other EVPs that were fairly clear on that night's recording. One of the most interesting was a male voice with a German accent. I had asked (for about the fourth time) if anyone was with me in the house.

"I am in love with the house," the man replied. Material bonds can create a situation that keeps us stuck to the Earth Plane. Certainly, loving a house could make one linger after death.

62 The Linda Lee

In another EVP a child is heard talking in the background to an older woman. The child asks, "Can he hear the tape?"

Who were all of these people? The voices did not sound like television or radio programs, so I ruled out recording analog signals on the tape. No one else (living) was staying there beside Willy and myself and the street was empty. I am always at odds with EVPs. Sometimes EVPs are great evidence of a haunting and other times they just lead off to a vague horizon of mindlessness. Knowing more about the house would help better understand any voices popping up on tape.

Because at the time of the initial investigation I was a long way away from writing this book, I just kept collecting data each time I stayed at The Linda Lee. When I sat down to write the story and finally uploaded the tapes, I realized I needed to dig a little deeper into the history of the house, so I had Archie fax me a copy of the house history. Working up a report of a long term ghost investigation can be a daunting task. There are many facets to consider and incorporate into each story, and history is something I feel very strongly about.

The Linda Lee, like many of today's B&Bs, was originally built as a private home. The house was constructed between December of 1871 and March of 1872 by a local builder named Richard C. Souder. Souder had been contracted by Peter McCollum, who was building houses in town on speculation.

The house was sold to John Henry Benezet, a local merchant in the hardware business. Benezet lived year-around in the house from December 5, 1872 until the fall of 1900, when he resided primarily in Philadelphia. Benezet died in 1921 and soon after his wife, Augusta sold the Cape May house to Adolph L. and Anna C. Tafel. Tafel was a wealthy pharmacist from Philadelphia with BOERICKE & TAFEL, a partnership with his brother-in-laws, Felix A. & Frank L. Boericke. According to Mike Conley's report, Adolph Tafel died at 725 Columbia while summering there in 1935. His wife Anna died in 1945, and the house was sold out of the family. The house saw a multitude of

Previous spread: The parlor at The Linda Lee B&B

ownership changes over the next sixty years until the Kirks bought the place.

Was Adolph Tafel the ghostly German voice on the tape? Unfortunately, when I checked old records, he was born in Pennsylvania, not Germany, so that (should have) ruled him out of the mix, at least for the moment. Maybe his family spoke German and he acquired an accent. I really do not know.

During the first investigation in January 2007, I asked for a sign that the ghosts were in the house; "three knocks," I requested. As I waited for the ghosts to make themselves known to me, I started hearing something banging about in the back of the house in the kitchen. It was not the three knocks I was hoping for, but I would follow the trail. Who knows, maybe they thought I said "three cooks."

As I moved into the kitchen, a voice says on the tape, "Here we are." Again, I did not hear it at the time, but I *could* sense something moving around me, however I was not sure who or what it was. Mediums can have off nights too.

Listening to the end of that original tape from January of 2007, I continued to ask my mundane mediumistic questions: "Who is here," "How long have you been here?" "Can you give me a sign please." All the words that must make the spirit world cringe, but a medium needs to know things when he or she is doing an investigation.

The last EVP on that tape is the voice of a woman exclaiming to the others, "I have to eat dinner."

Eat? Ghosts eat? I guess after all of that vacuuming one works up an appetite! Ghosts are a lot more like us than we think, and they may be living in a world very much like our own. Maybe, we're the ghosts and I am really just talking to some mediums on some other plane. The more I listen to EVP recordings, the more questions I have about how this whole ghost thing works. I try not to rely on EVPs. They just start to suck you in. Hours and hours of brain-numbing audio tape review. After a while, all that white noise just starts sound like static. Still, when there are results, it's like a high. I just can't pull myself away. This is why I have decided to use EVP evidence as one facet, not the only facet, of an investigation. I *am* a Medium after all. I look at it like this, instead of me versus the tape recorder, it's me with the tape recorder. I combine all of the evidence, psychic and physical and then I put the whole picture together.

In February of 2007, I returned to The Linda Lee. Stephanie's daughter Julie and her future husband Matt Scassero had now taken over as innkeepers, and both were very interested and open to the idea of ghosts. We settled in for the weekend and were joined by Gerry Eisenhaur, who came down from Boston to help us with the technical equipment. When I first did the walk-through of the Linda Lee, I felt Felicia's Room on the second floor was more active than the other rooms in the house. This is the room where guests had various experiences. We decided this would be the best spot for Gerry and his equipment. If something was going to be creeping down those narrow old servant's stairs, Gerry would be there with his gauges and meters in hand to greet them.

The first night, we decided to gather in the parlor for a little séance session. Gerry set up his camera and audio recording equipment and set out the EMF meters and temperature gauges. I positioned myself comfortably in a chair by the window and proceeded to adjust my energy to the energies of the house.

Right before I started officially channeling, Matt popped in to set the breakfast table. He did not know us too well at that point, but we invited him to sit in on the channeling—his first I believe.

It was February in Cape May, and, even though it was President's Day weekend, the town was quiet and deserted that evening. My feeling was that there were presences in the house, but they were distant. I put out a psychic line, though I was barely receiving anything. I felt that the ghosts were way up on the third floor—where Julie and Matt were now staying. I asked the ghosts to come down to us in the living room so we could communicate with them.

Opposite: Something has been using the old spiral servants' staircase that leads to the attic in Felicia's Room.

My feeling is that when I verbally ask, they sometimes can hear me, but many times they pick up a mental signal that the brain sends out in a thought wave, like a television signal combining both sound and visual images. My voice box sends out the sound wave and my brain sends out the visual idea. Ghosts have answered my verbal questions before on tape, and they have also sent me telepathic answers. Sometimes the psychic message will correspond with what is recorded on tape. Other times, I will either get a mental communication or an EVP communication, but not both.

I was having a tough time cracking into the ghost realm of this house that evening. I tried for almost ten minutes before I finally felt an energy shift. The room began to feel different to me, like people had started to arrive and the space became denser and more crowded. I can only describe the feeling of ghosts arriving as a *closeness,* where the walls seem to move in and the house energy closes in around me. It is like standing in a crowded subway car — people begin to crowd you and invade your personal space. Ghosts, with their far-flung energies, don't need to get as close to be on top of you. Just a ghost entering a room can give one a good mental nudge.

At nine minutes and thirty seconds into the channeling I sensed someone in the doorway of the parlor. I noticed the fringe on the lamp shade on the old stand lamp moving as if someone were running their fingers through the strings. A draft? The heat coming on? Perhaps. Perhaps not. I sensed the energy of a child in the room and asked it if it was with the house. I am now convinced that ghosts move around. A ghost need not have lived or died in a house to haunt it. He or she may have simply chosen to reside there for the moment or for a century. The living move around, so do the dead. I wonder if there are dead realtors in the ghost realm?

On the cassette tape, at almost exactly ten minutes a child's voice is heard in the white noise saying, "Daddy." It sounds like the voice of a three year old boy calling to his father. The EVP is "Class A" and you can hear it without headphones and understand exactly what it is saying. With headphones on — I could also hear faintly in the background, a man talking to someone else. I could not understand what he was saying. It was a "Class C" EVP. Inaudible and only heard with headphones. There are lots of Class C EVPs everywhere; they do not seem to yield much in the way of any value to an investigation. I think they are a form of ambient noise that exists everywhere.

Young children are known to be able to see ghosts and spirits of loved ones until about the age of three or four. Could the same apply to ghosts of children? Could they be more in touch with this side of the veil? After the child's arrival, the room started to paranormally percolate. Either the ghosts upstairs heard my request and were joining the party or I was about to join *their* party.

The EVPs started coming more heavily and faster on the tape. A man's voice says "Hello," in a rather metallic sounding tone. Another voice seems to say the word, "channel." Were they aware of what I was doing? Why can they see and hear us, but we need a recording device or a medium to hear them? Is the soul so evolved that when it leaves a body it activates some advanced form of senses? Are we much bigger and more complex creatures than we see in the mirror in the morning?

I asked the standard EVP gathering questions. When I asked can you tell me your name, the first word was, "John." Was this John Henry Benezet, the original owner present in the house? Benezet was a mover and shaker in Cape May and kept 725 Columbia as his permanent resident address, after relocating full time to Philadelphia, so he could vote on town issues. Could he be *that* connected to Cape May that he decided to stay?

My second standard question when I am doing an investigation is usually, "Can you give us a sign that you are here?" A throwback to the age of physical mediums and seances with levitating tables and floating trumpets, this question seems to really annoy ghosts.

The response on tape in a man's voice was, "Why do they do this?"

I don't know why I do it. It has been part of my repertoire since I started doing ghost investigations. Maybe I grew up watching too many haunted house movies on TV, or maybe I am just hoping for one more concrete piece of physical evidence that the ghost plane really exists. This question is rarely answered with the exception of an occasional bang or knock, which could very well be nothing more than a common house noise. I apologize to the ghosts for wanting a séance side show. I will try to control myself and not ask for any more signs — at least until the next book.

I wondered where Walter was in all this fuss and background conversation. Not once did the name Walter get mentioned on the tape or to me psychically. Did he move on? Was he at a wine tasting at one of the haunted restaurants in town? Stephanie had, on more than one occasion, told him to hit the road. Maybe he took the hint.

According to the records that Archie had, Walter was a much more recent owner of he house, having sold it in the early 1980s. I was not able to verify what happened to *that* Walter, and he may yet still be living. Still the occurrence of a ghost named Walter and a historical record for the house with an owner named Walter was, I think, more than just a coincidence. They also could be two completely unrelated Walters.

After about 20 minutes of little psychic activity, I finally began to sense a woman coming into the room. First, my left leg became cold and then I felt a tingling in my left arm. Ruling out any kind of circulation problems, I felt a ghost was near. This ghost had a female presence about it. I also psychically received the name "Mary."

The ghost gave me a feeling that she was a former housekeeper. This type of image just comes into my head. This type of psychic communication is not even so much a mental image as it is a planted memory — like something I always knew, but in reality is a completely new piece of information, put their by a ghost. Perhaps I am sharing their thoughts for a moment and my mind is trying to reference "who am I?"

Mary made her way around me, as if she were looking me over once or twice. The temperature around me began to drop and the EMF meter began to fluctuate. My cassette recorder momentarily stopped recording and then started again without anyone touching it. Mary's energy was affecting everything it touched, the living and the machine alike.

I could feel Mary moving in and joining my body. I want to stress I was *allowing* this spirit to come into my body—temporarily, to communicate. This is called *trance channeling*. It is extremely draining both physically and mentally, and I rarely do it anymore.

The entity called Mary came through slowly at first—almost in pain. She spoke with a definite Irish brogue and sounded like a woman in her sixties or seventies. It seemed to be difficult for her even to speak. When she did finally communicate verbally she spoke of seeing all of her friends grow old and pass on. She mentioned the house and having lots to do to keep things in order and that there were plenty of things for her to keep clean. When one of the crew asked her why she doesn't move on, she snapped, "I don't need you marchin' me to the grave!" She then abruptly stopped talking.

Ghosts seem to feel their lives have not ended with the death of their bodies. Crossing over to Heaven appears much more final to them. It is difficult for us, the living, to comprehend, since ghosts have a completely different vantage point from which to see their lives.

People are always telling me to get the ghosts to cross over. I can ask them to cross over, but that's about all I can do. If they are in the ghost realm, there is a reason. They have things to work out. I think it is another stage of a soul's journey. We *are* on a learning curve. I can only pray that the ghost is able to follow whatever path he or she has chosen and to see it to completion.

The body is only temporary lodging for the soul. Where we go from there depends on each individual path. Some people cross right over to the Other Side or Heaven, others stop somewhere in between, the place I call the *Ghost Realm* for lack of a better understanding.

Mary went on for another 30 minutes once she returned. She got stronger and louder as the night went on, finally leaving when she sensed my energy running low. Mary talked about creating what surrounds her with her own energy. That sometimes she cannot see past the walls of the house and sometimes she cannot even see past the room she is standing in. Other times, she recalled on a more elevated note, she could see things "as they were" when they were beautiful. I think she meant that occasionally the scenery changed back to how it was when she was alive.

She told us that the walls are just an illusion — like living in a bubble and not being able to see through to the other side of that bubble. I think she meant that our bodies are the bubbles — and while we are alive, we only see what is around us — nothing more. We can't think outside the bubble!

Several other entities tried to pop in from the street outside. They can sense my psychic energy and it seems to draw them closer to me. A child came through looking for its mother, a man from the street started to rant about this and that, someone named Walter came through talking about trying to drag a corkscrew upstairs and complaining that he kept dropping it (we later found a corkscrew on the third floor stairs about half way up) Finally, Dr. Arthur, a former owner of the house next door, came through introducing himself as someone who "doctors the dead." This voice was almost identical to an EVP that I would record upstairs in The Bacchus Inn later that year.

On that occasion, I had asked if anyone was in the room with us and the response on the tape in the same *old country doctor voice* was, "Who we got here? Just me and the maid." My channeled voice matched a disembodied voice on the tape. It seems that one's voice stays with them forever. Part of a soul's energy signature perhaps? Seems the good Doctor makes haunted house calls, but *that's* another story.

Throughout the channeling the group heard noises coming from the staircase out in the hallway. Clearly Mary had friends in the wings,

but they chose to remain silent and unseen. At one point Mary gestured to the wall facing the street and said that a group of "more than 30" had gathered outside and wanted to come in to speak through me.

Verizon I am *not*. This communication needed to end and it needed to end fast. My Spirit Guides who watch over me pulled the plug, causing Mary to fade back into the shadows of the ghost realm.

After I awoke from the trance and regained my physical and mental bearings on *this* plane, we decided to move upstairs and check on the random noises occurring on the higher floors. No one else was in the house at the time, so whatever was walking around up there was *not* breathing.

We stopped on the second floor landing with equipment in hand, while Gerry, Willy, Matt and I waited for something to give us a proximity signal. Within minutes phantom footsteps were heard on the stairs behind us leading to the third floor. They seemed to be coming toward us. The strongest energy, I sensed, was near the doorway of Sophie's Room, on the second floor near the front of the house.

We moved closer to Sophie's Room and opened the door. Gerry's EMF (electromagnetic field) meter, which usually fluctuates from zero to about 1.5, started to jump up into the teens. Gerry checked the walls and floor of the area because power lines are usually the source of EMF radiation in homes. Appliances are another source. He set the EMF meter on the floor in the doorway between Sophie's Room and the hallway where we were standing. The reading was about 0.4 which we felt was normal ambient energy.

Some paranormal researchers feel that areas that have high electromagnetic fields are more conducive to haunting phenomena. No one knows why this is true; it just seems to happen. Are the ghosts recharging their batteries by sucking energy from other sources?

I could feel something moving down the stairway from the third floor again and that feeling was followed by audible footsteps. I asked the ghost(s) to come forward and join us in the hallway. Suddenly the EMF meter spiked into the teens and then reset back to zero. On the

floor below was an exit light, but when checked with the same meter, there was very little in EMF readings. A small refrigerator nearby was also on the second floor, but that did not seem to be cycling or causing the meter to fluctuate. With EMF readings you really need to have a flat ambient reading and have it do something drastic, without moving the meter around. Drastic it was.

I asked the ghost(s) to please help us with a test. Would they please move into the area over the meter to help see if their energy would cause a spike. Within seconds, the meter peaked up around 31! I then told them to move back away from the meter and the meter reset to normal, about 0.5. We had a video camera on the meter the entire time and no one was moving. No one living that is. I knew we needed to rule out random chance, so I asked two more times for the ghost(s) to come and go. Both times the meter responded. Three times, on cue, an EMF meter jumped off the dial and then on cue went back to normal. That to me is more than a coincidence! No where else in the house did we get readings like this. As a matter of fact, I gave away my

EMF meter years ago because it only went off once at the Sea Holly Inn and never again. I never had much faith in EMF meters, but this time I must admit, *something* happened.

Right after that little show we heard footsteps retreating. The meter went silent and the house seemed to go to sleep. Had we worn out the ghosts?

Gerry spent the next two night's in Felicia's Room and woke up one evening to find his television had turned itself back on.

One of the most interesting experiences I had at the Linda Lee occurred during the first stay. Willy and I were in the newer addition on the back of the second floor. Felicia's Room with the servants' stairway was right behind the wall by the bed. Several times during the night we heard a door open and close, yet no one else was in the house and it was about 3 AM. We also heard footsteps on the stairs behind the wall. I awoke about 4 AM from a dream state to the sound of two people talking. I opened my eyes and the bedroom almost appeared on an angle. Something was just "off" about the feeling of the room. I had a very strong feeling I was in the same room, but in another time. Before I could get a fix, with the blink of an eye, the room changed back to normal and the voices disappeared. Had I experienced some sort of time warp?

As I mentioned in *Book 1*, one theory on hauntings is that they may be only a bleed-through from another plane of reality or another time. We could be experiencing sounds and movements from actual living people. It's one theory. My experience that night may have touched on that theory or I just might have been seeing what the ghosts were seeing, how things looked when they were alive. We really have no idea what they see, again only theories.

Julie and Matt Scassero are now married and continue to be the resident innkeepers at The Linda Lee. A radio turning itself off is about the strangest thing that has been happening recently. It seems that when they forget to turn the radio off, someone else remembers. Probably the same someone who does the ghost vacuuming.

If Walter has moved on or is never around when I need him, who is filling is in his place? Two female voices are heard on different tapes. Could this be the Benezet daughters (Florence and Isadora) or their servants? Who is the child who is heard in the background? Is it possible that these are only transient spirits having a short stay at the beach? Not every house is haunted and sometimes a ghost will move in for a short time and then leave.

As for Mary, the Benezets did have a servant named Mary Gibbs, but while I channeled an "Irish Mary," Gibbs is listed in the 1880 United States census as being born in Pennsylvania. The night of the channeling there was some question of where the Mary I was channeling worked. At one point she mentioned a house "down the block." When I first sensed the woman coming through in the channeling, she kept repeating, "they can't hear me." That woman seemed much fainter than the "Irish Mary" that I physically channeled.

With all of the great EVP activity I pulled from The Linda Lee tapes, not once did the ghost answer my questions about the Other Side, where they are or how or why they are there. There was only silence for an answer. Maybe that's how they want it. They always give me just enough evidence of the afterlife to let me know they are real, but not enough to create an airtight case that ghosts really exist. They taunt us with tidbits of their reality, then they pull back into silence.

I think that's exactly the idea. Why create too much interest and have hordes of people jumping onto the paranormal bandwagon and rushing at them with audio and video recorders and all kinds of probes, gauges and meters? Most of the adult ghosts I have encountered do not want to be bothered. Ghosts of children are a different story as you can see in some of the other chapters. Ghosts can be quiet when they want to go undisturbed; maybe giving away too many ghostly secrets would threaten their security or existence.

The Linda Lee is a wonderful place to stay, and the ghosts are typically quiet. I hope to eventually get to the bottom of who is haunting the place. The Linda Lee's ghosts are very tight-lipped about everything, it seems. Maybe they just don't want to — give up the ghost.

The Jacob Leaming House

SOMETHING OLD, SOMETHING NEW...
AND THEY'RE BOTH DEAD

Private Residence - 712 Columbia Avenue

"YOU have to meet our friends Audrey and Bill. You will love them!" exclaimed Stephanie Kirk on one of our visits to The Bedford. Audrey and Bill Schwab were the Kirk's old neighbors when they lived at The Linda Lee, and they had remained friends since. One thing lead to another, and I was invited to the Schwabs beautifully restored home on Columbia Avenue for cocktails on Halloween weekend. Luckily the wine was good and the house just happened to be haunted!

When I used to channel years ago at 710 Columbia, besides Walter roaming into my séances, a spirit of another man dropped by once or twice. He was checking on his old house next door, he said. Then as quickly as he arrived, he was gone. When I am in channeling mode, my energy must hook whatever ghosts or spirits are in the immediate area. Hmm, I thought, next door is haunted as well?

At the time the old Jacob Leaming house was being completely gutted and turned into guest apartments for summer rentals. Prior to the new owners taking over, the home was owned for many years by the Magee family. Robert C. Magee had written a wonderful pamphlet in 1987 on the history of Cape May called *Vintage Cape May: a Pictorial History of the Good Old Days*. Shortly before his death, he completed an updated and revised edition called *Vintage Cape May*. Both works included many rare old photographs taken by his family throughout their years in town. Sadly, Robert Magee died two days after completing his second work.

The house itself is a wonderful piece of Cape May history being built in the 1870s as a "railroad incentive house" by Jacob Leaming.

At the time, the Pennsylvania Railroad was offering "improvement tickets" to homeowners in Cape May. The company offered a free ticket to the head of any family, valid for rides between Philadelphia and Cape May for three years. The only catch was that the family had to build a house and spend at least $2,500 in the construction. Eventually business waned, and the Pennsylvania Railroad dropped the asking price to $2,000.

According to Magee's book, Jacob Leaming had only spent $1,800 to build his new home on Columbia Avenue, and he needed ticket for his son to go back and forth to the University of Pennsylvania. To get the ticket, he needed to spend another $200 on the house, so he had the carpenters return, lift the house up three feet and add a permanent wooden awning over the front porch. That, in addition to some other cosmetic renovations, brought the construction cost above $2000, and *that's* the ticket. In 2003, Bill and Audrey purchased the home and undid all of the "renovations" done by the previous owners. The house was restored to its original grandeur as a private home—and that's when all the fun began.

The Magee family lived in the home for many years and ran it as a boarding house called, The Belmont. After they sold the home, it passed to two gentlemen named Paul and Ed who started to gut the house and turn it into guest apartments. The conversion to apartment units was never completed as one of the men had died before the work was finished. After owning the house for only 18 months, the remaining partner decided to put the house back up for sale. Enter Bill and Audrey Schwab, who purchased the home in 2003.

When we arrived at the Jacob Leaming House in October of 2006, I did an initial walk-through of the home by myself. There were two distinct presences in the house. The first, Rachel came through and gave me the psychic impression she was cleaning the house. She was most likely a former servant. The next name that came through was Hannah. Hannah felt like she was from a different time period than Rachel.

I receive the impressions of some ghosts as a psychic package. I may sense old names and see bits and pieces of the past as if I were seeing through their eyes. These fragments of personal history combine to give me a sense of their character and era. If two or more ghosts are present from the same time period, I get a sense of a connection between them. In my mind I am transported back to whenever they lived. The experience happens in a flash, but gives me a good idea of whom I am dealing with.

Rachel and Hannah had a time/space between them, but they were now existing together in one house. If the two ghosts are from different time periods it makes my head spin. This energy mélange is like several songs playing at once. I am hearing all of the songs, but they are not flowing together.

I moved around the lower floor and found Hannah in the kitchen. I decided to check out the upper floors next. I told Audrey I was going upstairs, and she replied go right ahead. There was an EVP on the tape of a woman's voice saying, "He's coming up." There was also a man's voice saying something imperceptible back to her. The voices were sped up and sounded like they had been inhaling Helium. This is how many voices will come through on EVP recordings. The ghosts must be moving much faster than we are, voices included. Maybe this is why we rarely see them and when we do it is in the wink of an eye. Is this the normal speed of the soul and the body just anchors it and slows it down when we are in physical form?

On the third floor, Rachel and Hannah's energy was the strongest. Had they followed us up the stairs or was this their "living" quarters. I told Audrey not to give me too many details about the history of the house before I finished my search. She did say she thought she had seen the names Rachel and Hannah when Mike Conley had done the house history for them. She felt they may have been servants.

At that moment one of the doors on the third floor started to open by itself. I commented that every house in Cape May needs doors that open and close by themselves. A town has to keep up it's "most haunted" reputation you know!

As we moved down the stairs to the second floor, something told me to "stop" and stay where I was on the landing where the stairway turned. "Rachel is telling me — she said you've seen her — here."

"Oh my God! My daughter is going to cry!" Audrey exclaimed.

"Now you're a believer!" Bill added as the couple shook their heads in amazement.

"You just got me!" Audrey added.

As it turned out, unbeknownst to me, Audrey and Bill's daughter Holly had been dressing to go out with them to the Ebbitt Room one evening the previous spring. Holly moved across the hall to Audrey's bedroom to ask her if what she was wearing was alright for the restaurant. As she walked toward her mother she saw — something — standing above on the stairs, watching her. Holly had asked her mother if she just saw the figure, but Audrey had not.

"She is telling me she did not mean to frighten your daughter and that Hannah called her upstairs and she vanished."

Audrey said that was exactly what her daughter had seen, the ghost went up the stairs and vanished.

We moved to the back section of the second floor and the ghosts did not seem to follow. I felt the section had little or no energy and Audrey and Bill confirmed that it was part of the 1900 or 1910 addition to the house. The back wing was added at the same time and the house was also raised three feet off the ground. I had finished my house tour, and we decided to return to the living room. Audrey would now filled in some of the details of the house and related their experiences. I had asked her not to give me any information until after I did the walk through. With the exception of confirming the presence on the stairs, she did not want to influence my reading of the house.

There was a strong presence of a woman in the dining room, and I told Audrey I felt as if the woman had lived in that very room. Maybe she was a woman who used to stay there in the boarding house days, or she may have dated back to an older owner. I could sense the woman's radiant smile. She could see me. She knew what I was doing, and she was watching me like a loving grandmother watches her grandson at play. I felt she may have even been back visiting from Heaven, her presence was that strong. Much stronger and more focused than the two ladies haunting the third floor. The fact that I sensed her in the dining room gave Audrey a clue who the person might be.

Audrey told me a remarkable story that demonstrates how strong human will can be and how persistent a soul can be after death.

"We knew within two *days* of staying here overnight that there was something here — we knew there was something weird, within two *nights* of being here," Audrey started, "At the end of July, we had our burglar alarm go off — we have motion sensors. The burglar alarm company calls me and wakes me up at night and says we have an alarm coming through from your property. We're showing zone such and such, and I said what zone is that? They said, 'That's odd, it's your dining room—it's a motion.' So I said, 'where was my perimeter breached?'"

The police came and checked the house, and the alarm company could not find any perimeter breach. All was quiet at the house. As Audrey spoke with the dispatcher at the alarm company the dining room motion detector tripped once more.

"No one was in the house. The police never came into the house." Audrey had the man watching the property come and check through the house. Nothing was touched and everything was in tact.

"Your ghost is saying it was her," I told Audrey.

"It was her," Audrey replied.

It was not until two weeks later that Audrey thought she may have finally solved the mystery. She was reading a local newspaper when she spotted an obituary with a name that looked familiar. It was a former owner of the house. That woman had died on the exact same night that Audrey's alarm mysteriously went off!

"She came back once last time," Audrey added, "We hold her in the highest esteem. We thank her all the time, we feel she took great care of the home, and we are just taking over where she left off and want to keep the home in the very best condition."

Audrey and Bill even bought a small statue that is their tribute to the old owner. As Audrey pointed out the stone statue, I also noticed a large standing Dracula in the same room. It was a life-sized Halloween decoration with glowing red eyes that Audrey kept in the window for the holiday. I kiddingly said, "She was a vampire?"

As everyone laughed and Audrey said she meant the small statue of a lady on the shelf in the room, an EVP appears on the tape with a high pitched woman's voice saying, "I'm not a vampire!"

The ghostly woman in the dining room stayed for a while, watching me work and listening to Audrey and me talking. She complained to Audrey that she was not winding the clocks.

"That's true," Bill responded.

"I've got them chiming at 20 different times!" Audrey told her, trying to explain why she does not keep them wound.

The former owner, and there have been many in the house's 125+ year history, seems completely at peace with the work Bill and Audrey had done to her old home. I felt this woman was more of a spirit, who had returned from heaven to visit her old home. She is not earthbound like the other two ghosts, she comes and goes as she pleases.

Audrey told her she was welcome to come anytime and stay. It is wonderful to think that after we die, we are able to come back from Heaven and visit our old stomping grounds here on Earth. Just think, one could stay anywhere in Cape May — for free! However, I bet there is a long waiting list for the best rooms.

I have tried to find a Rachel or a Hannah associated with the original family who built the house. Jacob Leaming (1812-1888) married Malvina Eldredge (1823-1899) and they had three children; Theresa Eldredge (1843-), Amanda Melvina (1849-) and Jacob Spicer (1853-1935). No Rachels or Hannahs. The only Hannah, in the family, was Jacob Leaming's mother, Hannah Swain, but she died in 1857, long before the house on Columbia was built. It seems Rachel and Hannah may be former servants of the Leamings or even of one of the neighbors. They also may be from after the Leaming's tenure as owners of the house.

I found it quite interesting that Malvina Leaming was the daughter of Judith and William Eldredge, Jr. (1791-1832) of West Cape May. As you will read in my Ghosts of the West chapters, later in this book, the Eldredge clan is haunting up a storm on the other side of the tracks! Considering that Jacob Leaming died in this house, he and Malvina may have decided to stick around a bit and enjoy the family's paranormal picnic over in West Cape May.

Audrey and Bill Schwab are two of the most open-minded people I have met in Cape May when it comes to the subjects of ghosts. They love the idea that their house has a few "extras" on the third floor, and I think the ghosts enjoy their company as well.

In time, we may discover the true identities of Rachel and Hannah, but for now, they will continue to haunt the third floor of the Jacob Leaming house anonymously. Should you happen to be walking by 712 Columbia on a dark summer night, don't forget to wave hello to the ladies on the third floor. You might be surprised when you see something waving back.

Ludlam House

Ludlam House

A HOUSE FROM THE PAST
WITH ITS ORIGINAL CAST

Rental — 839 Kearney Avenue, Cape May

IT was a chilly late autumn morning in Cape May. Even with the rising sun, the late autumn sea breezes made it feel a lot colder. It was about 6:30 AM that November 9th in 1878 when Samuel Richard Ludlam, proprietor of The Ocean House on Perry and Washington Streets boarded a train for his winter home in Philadelphia. The Ocean House had closed for the season several weeks earlier, and Ludlam had finally gotten around to closing up his large summer home on the corner of Ocean Street and Columbia Avenue, the spot where the Humphrey Hughes B&B now stands.

About fifteen minutes after Ludlam boarded the train to Philadelphia, a worker on the roof of the Stockton Hotel spotted flames shooting out of the attic of the new wing of the Ocean House. Minutes later, Civil War hero Henry Sawyer, enjoying a morning cigar from the cupola of his Chalfonte Hotel, also spotted the flames and called in the fire alarm. The Great Fire of Cape May had begun. By evening, over 40 acres of prime summer real estate would be consumed. The fire left only fields of smoldering embers where great hotels like Congress Hall, Columbia House, Center House and The Ocean House once stood.

Ludlam became the prime suspect, having recently heavily insured his hotel. Some speculated that a slowdown in business in Cape May, caused by the financial recession of the time, was the perfect excuse for Ludlam to stoop to arson to get back his invested monies in the form of an insurance settlement. Ludlam was arrested in Philadelphia and brought to trial in Cape May. The jury, however, found him not guilty on the charges of arson. The evidence brought forth by the prosecution was circumstantial and not enough to convict him. In the end, the fire department took the blame for faulty hoses and poor equipment. Ludlam was free to continue to do business in Cape May.

As for that summer home on the corner of Ocean and Columbia, a strange thing happened during the 1878 catastrophe. The great fire roared around the house and scorched three sides of the building, but the old mansion escaped the blaze with only a few burn marks. It was almost like something was watching over the house. *Something* was and still *is* — and this is *their* story.

For many years, I stayed with Walt and Patti Melnick at their former Sea Holly Inn B&B on Stockton Avenue. In the summertime, parking in Cape May is at a premium. Many times there would not be a space available near the Sea Holly, and I would have to park one block back on Kearney Avenue. I am not quite sure when I noticed Ludlam House, but I am sure it noticed *me* right away. When a collection of ghosts have been in one place for such a long period of time, they create a group consciousness that radiates energy.

My theory is that ghosts, fields of energy with a consciousness operating in the same space for a long time, start to *mesh* their energies. There is no physical presence, just the remaining energy the body has left behind. I think that energy can mix. Various ghosts' personalities can also mix together. The energy in a spot with multiple personalities is much stronger than where there is only one ghost.

Walking by a psychic hot spot like Ludlam House is like walking past a bakery for a medium. Something keeps drawing us in. It is usually a positive feeling, one of happiness and a general sense of well being. This type of energy is like a psychic magnet for living intuitives.

Like many summer homes in Cape May, Ludlam House has seen its share of owners, and their families come and go. The house was built around 1875 on the site of what is now the Humphrey Hughes B&B. When I first stayed at Ludlam House I was under the impression that he had owned the home until his death in 1900. With the help of Devra Bennung, one of the more recent owners of the house, and Cape May historian Jim Campbell, I was able to finally piece together the correct chain of ownership of the house.

After the great fire and the accusation of Ludlam having started it, he decided to sell the home and move elsewhere. Samuel R. Ludlam sold the property at Ocean & Columbia to Samuel Nathan on December 2, 1879 (Deed book 45, page 489.) Samuel Nathan then sold the property to native Irishman Nicholas J. Griffin and his wife Rosi on October 19, 1889 (Deed Book 87, Page 439).

While little is known about Nathan, Griffin's efforts to upgrade the old home were well documented in the local papers. Here is the article as it appeared in the February 5, 1890 *Cape May Star and Wave*:

"Nicholas J. Griffin will have one of the handsomest summer residences in town when it comes from the hands of Joseph I. Williams who designed the improvements and superintended its construction. It is practically a new house.

Its former owner would scarcely recognize it since the alterations have been carried out by the builder. The include a commodious square tower on Ocean Street front; porches around three sides; increased cellar room; modernizing working parts of the house; elevation of the whole building; grading up sidewalks; and other extensive betterings all over the building.

Inside there will be hard wood finishing in chestnut and ash in all the fifteen rooms.

From the front tower a commanding view of the sea, Columbia Avenue and Ocean Street may be had. The plumbing will include all modern appliances of luxury.

The cost of this important betterment will be $3,500.00 a sum which seems small when the extent of work is considered.

Mr. A. C. Gile will do the decorating outside and in. When the house comes from his hands, owners of other Ocean Street cottage holdings will have to look to their laurels or they will be distanced in the modern race for the best.

Mr. Griffin is to be warmly congratulated on the choice of location and in the substantial character of his summer home completed by Mr. Williams."

The Griffin House was one of the showplaces in Cape May. It is the next few years of the house's history that get a little bizarre and so far are still a bit sketchy.

Several years before Griffin did his renovations, Richard Campion, a pioneer in worsted yarn from Philadelphia, began purchasing properties in Cape May. Campion purchased two properties at Kearney & Jefferson, one in September 7, 1880 (Deed book 157, Page 318) and the other in August 15, 1911 (Deed book 270, Page 26). Another deed book with a Campion deed (Book 63, Page 448) was out being rebound when Jim Campbell tried to research the house for me.

Devra Bennung told me that around 1907 Griffin sold the house to Richard Campion, and it was Campion who had it moved to its present location on the corner of Jefferson and Kearney. She told me a woman came up to her home in the mid-1960s and recalled watching the house moved on logs, pulled by horses and mules! Imagine moving an entire mansion on logs — all the way up Columbia Avenue and down Jefferson to Kearney! I guess Campion really liked the house.

Why someone would sell *just the house* I have still not been able to ascertain. That property on Ocean Street is certainly no shabby piece of real estate. Once the house was moved the current Humphrey Hughes home was erected on the same site.

Richard Campion (1842-1921) summered in the home with his wife Susan Hulme Grundy Campion (1857-1900) and their daughter Susan Grundy Campion Emack. After his wife died around 1900, Campion and his family continued to summer in Cape May at the old house until 1921 when Richard Campion died in Philadelphia at the age of 79 on September 13, 1921. He left the property to his daughter Susan C. Emack who, with her husband James H. Emack, sold the property to Henrietta Bunting Cope, wife of Porter Cope of Philadelphia, on December 14, 1925 (Deed book 415, Page 490.) The house next went to Cope's daughter, Millicent Cope Twining in 1952. In 1965 Twining sold the house to Devra and Karl Bennung who in turn sold the house to Nicholas and Cathy Force.

Ludlam House, as I will refer to it in this story even though it has had many owners, is a grand Victorian in all senses. The house stands apart from its neighbors. It actually dwarfs most of the houses in the immediate neighborhood. The magnificent 12 foot high wrap around porch is *the* best porch in Cape May, hands down. Located two blocks from the Ocean and set up about 12 feet above the ground, the view is not too bad either. At one time, when the area was called Frog Hollow and was a filled in swamp, Ludlam House must have had a magnificent view of the ocean. Today, only the third floor bedrooms can peer out to sea.

I could always sense people inside the house as I walked by the front picket fence and stopped to gaze up to the third floor tower. Many haunted places will not give off a strong enough energy for a psychic medium to be able to detect anything from the street, but Ludlam House, like a few other high energy places in town, gives off its own energetic welcome.

A few years ago I noticed a Dellas rental sign in the front yard of the house and I decided to give my friend Kim Dellas, a lifelong resident of Cape May and one of the area's best realtors, a call. I spoke to her husband Paul Andrus about seeing the house for a potential summer rental. Paul met my partner Willy and me on the front porch and gave us a tour of the old place.

Standing on the front porch alone is enough to make anyone want to rent Ludlam House! This section of town is much quieter and more peaceful than the main downtown areas. You could start rocking and fall asleep for hours without anything waking you up.

The first thing that struck me about Ludlam House was the painting on the interior walls. The ceiling in the living room was painted with a massive garden motif and that design, so popular with the Victorians of the day, continued around the walls of the staircase up to the third floor. My first thought after seeing the historic interior of the house was, "How did this house get under the radar of the historic groups in town?" As I learned later from Devra Bennung, who was a font of information on her old home, when she and her husband lived there it was anything but "under the radar!" The Bennungs were on the MAC house tours all the time and had been written up in several publications. Isn't it funny what a few years can do? Today, very few people in town know anything about the house.

That summer we opted for a rental in West Cape May, but I returned to look at Ludlam House again, this time accompanied by Kim Dellas. Kim and I tried to count how many rooms and baths there were, as the house seemed to stretch in all different directions. At one point I poked my head inside a darkened closet on the stairway landing only to see a doorway hidden a few feet down a short dark hallway *inside* the closet. I could see light coming through the doorway; I thought of Ira Levin's *Rosemary's Baby* apartment interior shots, with hallways inside closets. Feeling like Rosemary Woodhouse, I walked slowly through the darkened hallway trying several doors until one opened revealing an entire back section of the house! It was like a house within a house and quite beautifully decorated at that!

I had stumbled what I thought were the maid's quarters, but as I would learn from the house's previous owner, it was the original house that Ludlam had built. Everything forward was created or expanded by Griffin. As I looked through the many additional rooms, I tried to reason in my mind how mules and logs could have moved this entire house across town. I still can't figure it out.

Willy and I decided we would rent the house for Halloween weekend when I would be doing all of my tours, and we would have a big Halloween party for everyone involved in my two books. Unfortunately, Kim got back to me later with the bad news—Ludlam House had *no* heat. It was only a summer home to start with, and no one had ever used it in the winter months. It is against the law for anyone to rent an unheated building after October 14th. So we did the next best thing. We rented it for a week in the summer.

That fall, I was in the Winterwood Gift Shop, checking to see if they needed more of my *Ghosts of Cape May* books. As I spoke to the clerk, a soft spoken woman tapped me on the shoulder and introduced herself to me as Cathy Force, the current owner of Ludlam House. What a great coincidence I told her. We chatted briefly about the house and I carefully broached the subject of ghosts, not sure at the time how she was with the idea. I told Cathy that I could sense multiple presences in the house when I did my walk through.

"Oh we definitely have something in there," she replied looking to the friend she was with who gave a nod and a verbal confirmation.

I told Cathy I would like to stay in the house for a week and investigate the ghosts and write a story about it; she was in agreement.

In July of 2006, we arrived at 839 Kearney for a magnificent week at the shore and a trip into the paranormal world that we never expected.

Willy and I had invited our dear friend Kathy DeLuccia to come along with us for the week. Kathy had seen the house a few weeks earlier on a day trip to Cape May and was excited about being able to spin her wool (she is big into spinning and weaving) on the wonderful front porch in the ocean breeze. We had no idea at the time that Richard Campion had been in the business of spinning wool! Just another strange Cape May coincidence.

We had several other friends coming down for the latter part of the week to join us for my book signing and dinner at Congress Hall, but I wanted to keep the house clear and quiet so that I could get to know the ghosts. For this time it would be just me, Willy and Kathy.

I am sure all of my other friends, who had to pay to stay at other places in town, were wondering why I was renting a "sleeps twenty" mansion for only three people. However, I wasn't just counting *living* people staying in the house — so the house, as it turned out, was already *quite* crowded.

We pulled our van into the back and parked on the lawn as instructed. We took turns carrying luggage around to the front of the house. Once everything was organized by the front door I got the key out of my pocket and pulled open the large screen door. As I reached with the key to open one of the old double front doors... both doors *blew* open! I had not yet unlocked them.

"That is *so* "cheap Hollywood haunted house movie," I thought to myself. That doesn't actually happen in real life hauntings — does it? Maybe the ghosts have been watching too many B movies. Both doors opening *was* a bit of a wild thing to experience — I must admit.

Once inside we gave Kathy DeLuccia her official tour of the house. While only the front section of the house was the actual rental, Cathy Force had agreed to leave the back section open of the house for my investigation. We finally made our way to the third floor tower room which is a small bedroom with windows on three sides, a great cross breeze and a fabulous view of the ocean.

"I'll take this one!" Kathy exclaimed and proceeded to set her luggage down on the floor.

"You can have the entire third floor," I told her as I attempted to turn on some lights and a fan.

"This light isn't working," Kathy called to me as I nosed around the other rooms.

"Neither are any of these," I called back. It seemed the power on the third floor was out, with the exception of one ceiling fan and a wall light fixture. Kathy did not seem to mind, and we lent her one of our flashlights to navigate at night and use the darkened bathroom. I would call Cathy in the morning and ask her where the breaker panel was located. I thought, the previous renters had tripped the circuit on the third floor by plugging in too many hair dryers or something.

The three windows in the third floor bedroom were wide open creating a wonderful view *with* ocean breezes included. As Kathy went toward the front window to look out at the view, a bouquet of artificial flowers, firmly planted in a vase in front of the window, leaped out of the vase and landed on the dresser top—below the window ledge. Kathy picked them up and put them back in the vase. A gust of wind blew them toward Kathy—one more time. We found it odd that the windows had been open all day and the flowers had just decided to take flight upon Kathy's arrival into the room. I was standing behind her and witnessed the entire event.

Kathy and I looked around the rest of the third floor. She decided to take the front tower room so we returned there to find the flowers were now *on her bed*—on the pillow to be exact. If they had blown there, the wind would have first had to blow them into the room and then a crosswind would have had to take them sideways to the bed. Highly unlikely we thought. It was more likely a "welcome message" from some unseen friends in the house. At least they were friendly.

I chose the tower room on the second floor directly below for my sleeping quarters. I had fallen in love with the room when I first visited the house. According to Devra Bennung, Millicent Cope Twining had told her it was Griffin's Chapel. It certainly had the look of a chapel with its beautiful Gothic shaped windows on three sides filled with rich shades of deeply colored stained glass and surrounded by dark

The paranormally charged jumping BOO-quet

wood paneling. There was also an old servant's call button on the wall that I would imagine was used when guests relaxed for the evening in the beautifully wainscoted room in the evenings. This "chapel room" has an energy all to itself, and I felt very comfortable every time I entered the room. It was dark, but the energy was very bright.

We settled in for our first evening in Ludlam House. After Willy's brother Al and sister Leli, along with Al's children, had spent the day with us visiting sites in Cape May, Leli decided she would love to stay a few nights. I relented to have another guest — I set her up in the bedroom on the first floor. After a long day of sightseeing, we all turned in for the night. At least the living members of the house turned in for the night — the dead must have had insomnia.

Ghosts do most of their business at night. With no physical body to tire, they can pretty much stay active 24/7. I had just started to fall asleep when I heard a door creak open out in the hallway. I had left the double doors to the library open as Willy had taken refuge in an

adjoining bedroom, with more privacy and a bigger bed. He wanted me to be within earshot in case anything happened.

I thought it might be Kathy roaming about the third floor, trying to find the bathroom in the dark. The noises were followed by footsteps. I sat up in bed, cricked my head around the corner of the doorway, and listened into the hallway. The footsteps (there were several sets of them) were coming up from downstairs. As I listened I realized that the footsteps were stopping at the landing three quarters of the way up, where the doorway was to the back of the house. The footsteps stopped, and I finally fell asleep.

Shortly after falling asleep, one of Cape May's famous nocturnal thunderstorms blew in from the bayside. Since I come from a gene pool that fears everything that can possibly happen to you, including being struck by lightening, I got up and attempted to close the windows. As I struggled with the old windows to get them to cooperate, (they were swollen in place) I heard two women talking in the house. The words were not audible, but the voices speaking were definitely female. Had Kathy gone down to close windows and awakened Lel? The voices stopped, and I thought it was Kathy talking in her sleep, as she was on the third floor but slept with her door open. I could see light coming from the top of the stairs, but no movement. As it turned out, Kathy fell asleep with the light lit.

The next morning, Lel asked me who I was talking to in the middle of the night.

"Me?" I replied.

"Yes," she told me, "I heard a man and a woman talking in the living room and outside my door and I assumed it was you and Kathy," Lel continued.

I was not the only one hearing voices that night. Willy said he also heard voices, but thought they might have been outside. Lel said she ruled out that possibility having gotten up from bed to hear what direction they were coming from. Her bedroom windows on the side

Previous spread: The Chapel Room on the second floor.

of the house were open, but the voices were coming from *inside* the house.

Sunday morning I decided to sleep a little later than normal. Kathy and Willy, who get up with the roosters, had joined Lel on the porch for coffee. I went in for my normal morning shower when I felt something strange in the large, unused bedroom on the second floor. I had been using the bath adjoining that room since we arrived and had felt nothing in the bedroom itself. Now *something* was in there with me! I went into the bathroom and closed the door. I finished washing the shampoo out of my hair and felt a breeze come past me in the shower. I looked through the glass stall to see that the bathroom door was now *open*. (Don't you hate when that happens?) I turned off the water and dried myself and heard Kathy, Lel and Willy still laughing and talking downstairs on the front porch. Knowing it was either the wind or a ghost, I closed my eyes and turned on my full psychic senses.

In the doorway, for a moment, I saw a middle-aged woman holding the hand of a young girl with blond curly hair. When they realized I could see them (with my mind,) they vanished into some other dimension out of my psychic sight. I think ghosts need to get closer to view or interact with the living. They may truly be nearsighted. This is just what these two curious ghosts were doing. I made a note of it and told the others what I had just seen.

On Monday Willy drove his sister back up to catch the train to New York from Atlantic City. He had spent the morning searching for his sandals that had mysteriously disappeared from the house. I had also had a beach towel vanish from the second floor bedroom rocker. I had been drying it in the ocean breeze that was coming in the window. Not able to locate his sandals, Willy slipped on a pair of shoes and went off with Lel to Atlantic City.

Kathy sat on the porch gaily spinning her alpaca wool into thread on her old spinning wheel. I decided after two nights of darkness, I would call Cathy Force and have her tell me where the breaker panel was. Cathy told me that the panel was in the cellar, under the house. She mentioned it was quite a mess and vast, and we joked about me not going down there — alone. It also happened to be the former servants' quarters.

I hung up the phone with Cathy Force and went onto the porch to get Kathy to accompany me down to the old cellar.

"I have to get my shoes," Kathy mentioned, getting up from her chair on the porch. "I think I left them up in my bedroom."

I headed to the back of the house to get a flashlight when I heard a crash and Kathy's yell. I headed back around the corner to see Kathy halfway up the stairs, staring in disbelief at her high-heeled shoes that had just *fallen from above,* hitting the steps behind her! No one else (living) was in the house at the time, yet Kathy's shoes made a fast airborne trip from the third floor to the first floor and landed right behind her on the steps. Now *that's* room service!

Kathy and I then headed up to the third floor to test the idea. Holding my sandals, one at a time, I dropped them through the opening between the staircases. It was possible for someone to bounce a shoe off the second floor staircase railing and direct a shot right onto the first floor stairs. The problem was — there wasn't anyone on the third floor at the time!

Shoes firmly strapped to our feet, Kathy and I headed for the cellar. We would have to enter through an exterior door as the interior cellar door was now sealed up behind the refrigerator in the kitchen. When we finally found the right key to the padlock on the old cellar door.

Kathy and I made our way into the cellar. Cathy Force was right. It was vast — and a mess. It was also *jumping* with psychic activity! I could sense a wall of ghostly energy go right through us as we made our way down the dimly lit old hallway. Crumbling plaster and lathe walls indicated the ground level basement was once an elaborate layout of hallways and rooms for a staff long gone — at least long dead.

We found the room Cathy had told us about, luckily not too far into the cellar and I opened the breaker box. Cathy had just had all of the electrical fixtures replaced and was surprised something would have tripped one of the new breakers. To our surprise, the breaker for the

The former servants' quarters — now the dark and creepy cellar.

third floor was not tripped, it was *turned off*. I turned it back on and waited a moment. It stayed on this time. It did. Kathy and I gathered our courage and decided to investigate a little deeper into the cellar.

The rooms continued and the cellar got darker as we moved away from the daylight coming in the back cellar windows. We got as far as a second hallway when something stopped me in my tracks. It was a strong feeling that something did not want us to go any further. We were intruding on its space. It felt like the presence of an older man. I gracefully said, "Thank you for letting us look." Kathy and I exited quickly, locking the door behind us.

I returned upstairs to find messages from Willy on my cell phone. Our van's transmission had decided to give out in Atlantic City but, luckily, Willy was able to drive back to Exit 9 on the parkway and call for help. Kathy and I, without a car, could not do a thing to help him. So, we waited on the porch for news.

During our wait, Kathy wondered aloud if the ghosts couldn't help find Willy's missing sandals. With that, we heard a loud thump come from inside the house. We rushed in to find everything the same as we had left it. That is until we noticed the basket on the stairs that usually holds mail was now holding Willy's missing sandals!

Willy rejoined us that evening, courtesy of the towing company, to continue our "relaxing" vacation. $2,500 later, our van also returned to us so we could get back home.

I decided to call Cathy Force again and report to her that the lights were back on, and give her a full run down of the paranormal activity. We were to stay a week and this was *only* the third day of our visit!

Hearing about the paranormal events, Cathy told me what she had experience after first buying the house three years ago.

"They kept slamming doors on me." Cathy told me. She felt they were friendly, but the ghosts wanted to let her know she was not in the house alone.

It was not until I described the little girl with blond curls and the older woman holding her hand that Cathy burst out with excitement on the phone.

"Go upstairs — in the bedroom I think — there is a picture I brought in to the house of a little girl!"

I walked upstairs and found the oval picture hanging in the hallway. Cathy told me she purchased it after hearing from other tenants about a little girl with blond hair. It seems renters were in the house with their family and the mother of the family was putting her baby to bed in the bedroom where I had seen the pair earlier. The mother described a young child with blond curly hair, standing in the room with an older woman who may have been her mother. The tenant did not think they were ghosts, instead she thought they were staying in the back of the house. When the mother turned to put her baby down, the ghosts vanished instantly. No one else was in the house. The woman realized she had just seen two ghosts. After hearing the story and re-

A picture bearing a strong likeness to "Sophie," Ludlam House's child ghost hangs against the old painted wall on the second floor.

ceiving other reports, Cathy thought she would add the picture to the house for the ghostly little girl. Cathy Force is very open to the idea of ghosts and spirits, as she is a Reiki Master and very in tune with various energies outside the normal senses. She is also a great person... and that helps a lot!

Cathy told us other guests in the house had things go missing. A little girl's pair of jeans vanished, and other things would vanish and then turn up months later. I hope that my beach towel will return by next summer! The ghosts are very active in this old house. I started to piece together the Ludlam family history, with the help of my friend Jim Campbell. During my encounter with the ghosts, I was given the name, "Sophie." However, according to Jim's research, Ludlam did not have a daughter named Sophie. Was Sophie the older woman or was the child just using a made up name after all these years? There would be one sure way to find out. A séance was in order.

I arranged for the séance to be held in the front parlor on the last day of our stay. I had asked my friend Rick Borutta to join us. Rick is a filmmaker who does documentary work, and I have been toying with the idea of creating a series of DVDs about my investigation in Cape May. Our friend Sandy also joined us and acted as the sound person for Rick.

I agreed to start the interview part of the filming in the house that afternoon. For the official evening séance, I had invited the Ludlam House's current owner, Cathy Force, to join us. However, the ghosts decided to arrive well ahead of Cathy and the dead quickly rearranged my schedule, once again.

We set up Rick's video camera in the front parlor. I sat in a rocking chair and watched him adjust his equipment. He attached the TV in the house to his setup and used it to playback what he was shooting.

I had a thought. I have run cassette tapes in haunted places, and have captured several EVPs (electronic voice phenomenon) or ghost voices on tape. I had never tried ITC *(Instructional Transcommunication.)* The theory about ITC is that ghosts and spirits from another dimension or plane of existence can communicate through television. More precisely, when a video camera is pointed directly at a television monitor and set to record with the video monitor set to play what is being recorded, as endless loop is created. Within this loop, pictures sometimes appear on the television screen. Researchers have claimed to see faces of people who have departed and of unknown sites, all appearing on the monitor.

I asked Rick if he could set up and ITC loop while I would channel the ghosts in the house. Rick was unfamiliar with the idea but obliged and I began to relax into a trance channeling state. Apparently, while I was in trance several of the house's unseen occupants came through me and used my voice box to communicate with my group that was present. This is nothing out of the ordinary. I have trance channeled before with good results. It is not something I do often, but this house was different, it had multiple energies that might be reached through a deep trance channel.

I focused on the energies of the house and asked the ghosts for a sign to tell me where they were at that time. A dull thump was heard coming from the floor. I asked two more times. Each request was followed by a loud, dull thump. From our earlier experience in the vast cellar under the house, I knew that the thumps were coming from the old servants' quarters below. I had a strong sense of a presence when my fiend Kathy and I had gone looking for the breaker panel earlier that week. Now the directional rapping confirmed for me that these ghosts might have been former servants of the Ludlam family.

As I channeled, the ghost of the young girl came through. She cried for her mother causing my voice to hit high notes that I later heard on the tape. The amazing thing about trance channeling is that many of the voices sound nothing at all like the voice of the channeler. As I mentioned in part one of this article, I was given the name "Sophie" for one of the ghosts. We think the young girl might be Sophie, but she did not respond to that question.

Sophie was lost. The young child cried, wanting her doll returned. Someone had buried her doll, she told us. We later ascertained that this meant she had died and the doll was buried with her. As a ghost, she would have left her body upon dying. She probably did not recognize herself when viewing it from her spectral body. She *did* recognize the doll and wanted it back—from the grave. Sorry Sophie, not today.

Another unidentified male spirit then came through. It sounded as if he had worked for the owners of the house in the early days and he and a few others had stayed on. He talked about keeping the house up and things in need of repair.

While watching the ITC video which ran along with an audio of my trance channeling, we all noticed a most amazing coincidence. Each time a different entity would speak through me the color and imagery

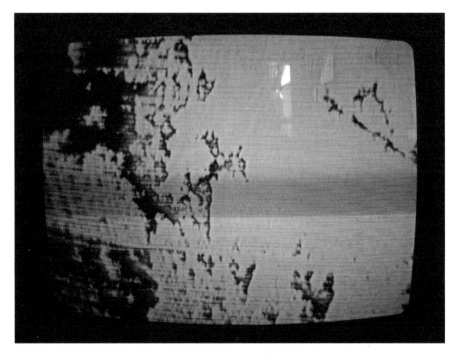

ITC Image captured by Ric Borutta at Ludlam House. Notice the man's head in the upper left part of the screen and the girl's face lower right.

on the screen would change. At first, the images looked like inkblots. I was careful that we all did not start giving our own "Rorschach test" interpretation of what we "thought" we were seeing. Soon a pattern developed however, and the "inkblots" started to morph into a landscape.

When we reviewed the section of the tape where I channeling the male entity, the scene looked like a long beach with dunes, grass and an ocean. That picture played for a few minutes. It reminded me of the movie *Contact* with Jodi Foster, where she arrives on some distant planet on a surreal looking beach. Was the spirit trying to send us an image of where he was? Was this Heaven or another plane of existence like our own? On the other hand, were we seeing old Cape

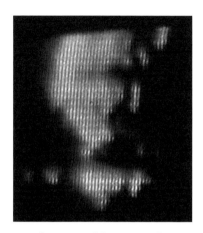

Close-up of the man's face

May? Before we could get a grasp on the picture, the images began to morph again. In the upper left hand corner, a white face of an older man appeared and seemed to be looking right at us. After that point, the video images shifted to muddled static.

Coming from a communications background in college, this idea seemed a little far-fetched. The thought of filming a TV screen, and recording a loop, was a little too *Dr. Who* for me. I was sure there was some explainable reason why the picture would look like it did when it was looped back on itself repeatedly. I checked out other of ITC sites on the web. I could not find too many images as intensely real as the ones we had recorded.

At that time, my channeling energy was running full tilt. I know I can generate some strong kinetic energy. That energy can kick up a haunting into full gear, but I am not sure *what* to make of this first attempt at communicating with the spirits over the television!

We decided to break, after reviewing the tapes for more ITC evidence. It was our last day in Cape May, and we had other friends in town who were missing our company. We returned to the house later that night and were joined by owner Cathy force, her daughter Erika and Erika's mother-in-law, Suzanne. Along with Rick, Sandy, my partner Willy and friend Kathy DeLuccia the group became too large to

Close-up of the girl's face

108 Ludlam House

Craig channeling the ghosts of Ludlam House — hey somebody's got to do it.

conduct a quiet little séance. I opted instead for another channeling session.

That evening, I slipped into a trance state once more. The ghost of the child returned, with her older male friends. Up to this point, we have been calling the child, *Sophie* because we were given that name psychically at the beginning of the stay. Sophie may have been the name of the ghostly woman, I saw with the child earlier.

It is almost impossible to sense a ghost's, unless I can reach that ghost in a direct trance state. If I sense a name during an investigation, that particular name might be from one of the ghosts who are present. It may even be something one of the ghosts is saying. For the sake of this book, I will refer to the little girl as *Sophie*.

Sophie talked about trying to pick flowers outside the house, but the ghosts kept pulling her under the house and keeping her there. We later interpreted this as the older members of the group trying to keep Sophie from causing a disturbance in the house. Sophie was still very much the personality of a young child, even though she was probably an old ghost.

There was a certain "feel" to the older ghosts of the house. They spoke of trying to keep the house the way they liked it and to maintain it for the owners. It seemed as though the staff had remained behind, but the old owners had moved on to Heaven. In the ghost world, you have a mix of different personalities with one thing in common; none of the personalities want to move on. Only one male voice talked about wanting to be "freed," while the rest were happy to look after the house and Sophie, I assume.

While the group listened intently to my channeling, several thumps and bangs, were heard upstairs in the bedroom above us. After the channeling was over, it seemed Sophie and some of the ghosts decided to give us a little show. As we made our way up the winding stairs to the second floor, we found, in the bedroom directly above the channeling below, draws had been taken out of the dresser and stacked perfectly on top! The picture of the little girl with blond curly hair, that Cathy Force had bought for the house after renters had reported seeing the same ghost that I had, was now in the rocking chair in the same room—as if to say, "It's me!" The energy was completely benevolent and felt like a child was playing tricks on its parents. I think Sophie is not only very attached to the house but also identifies with owner Cathy Force as a mother figure.

Cathy told me when she first saw the house she fell in love with it. During the channeling, one of the spirits came through and provided a further confirmation—Cathy had been living in the house in a previous lifetime! It made sense to Cathy at the time. She told me she always loved Cape May (Don't we all?) and that she also loves the house and was thrilled when it finally came on the market for sale. I think we all have many incarnations on this Earth plane. Sometimes we choose the same place to reincarnate because we love the experience so much. I am sure I have been around the spirit block in Cape May many times myself!

After we left Ludlam House, we all had the same experience. I felt almost depressed when I came back home. My partner Willy was also very down, and it had nothing to do with vacation being over because we were heading out to another venue the following week. Kathy DeLuccia also felt "flat" and Rick and Sandy echoed the same feelings. What had happened to us? My theory is that we were in a very "high energy" location where two planes meet very easily. The higher vibrational energy had us both charged up and relaxed. When we left, we broke the connection and went into energy withdrawal. I have not had this happen to me in a long time, but it has happened before. Ludlam House just had a soothing energy about it. I can see why the ghosts want to stay—the place is like an energy spa!

With any ghost investigation, I try to incorporate some of the history of the place I am writing about. Knowing the history of a house can help to pull the entire paranormal puzzle together.

As I mentioned in the beginning of this chapter, the original owner of the house, was Samuel R. Ludlam, was accused of setting the Great Fire of 1878. He had summered in Cape May with his wife Elmira Mecray Ludlam and their children. After the séance and investigation, I tried to find a "Sophie" in the Ludlam line, but there was none connected with Samuel R. Ludlam's family. Ludlam did have a young daughter Cora, who seems to have died as a teenager, but no Sophie. His other children, Henry, William, Thomas and A. Marcy Ludlam, all lived into adulthood. Elmira and son A. Marcy went on to run The Virginia Hotel on Jackson Street until A. Marcy's death in 1915.

Can there be multiple generations of ghosts in a house? Absolutely. All too often people make the mistake of thinking ghosts have to be hundreds of years old. It is possible to have a ghost in your house that is only a week or a month or a few years old. The Victorians do not have exclusivity on ghosts. Originally I thought it may be the Ludlams haunting the house, but after putting the early history together, it would seem unlikely that Ludlam would return to a house he had given up in life. It seemed to me that the Griffins were more likely to be haunting as they had really built the house that stands today.

Willy Kare (left) shoots a video as Gerry Eisenhaur (right) scans the steps below with the Flir Thermal Camera and spots ghostly footprints.

I could find no other information about the Griffins other than they had a son named David. What about the Campions? Mrs. Campion died early in their ownership of the house. Was Susan Campion the middle aged woman I had seen?

Much of the energy of the house is also coming from under the house, in the former servants' "wing." Maybe the ghosts are all former staff members and none of the original owners are doing the haunting. Only time, and more research, will help to shed light on the ghosts of Ludlam House.

We made one last visit to see Cathy Force during our photography shoot for Book 3. This time I brought in Gerry Eisenhaur, who had never had the chance to get his technical hands on the house. We rented a fancy-smancy Flir Thermal Imaging Camera and brought that along with us. The camera proved to be of real value on this trip.

It was able to photograph and document patches of heat in several spots on the floor of the house where there had been no living presence.

At one point during another channeling, I conducted in the parlor, footsteps could be heard on the stairs. The Flir Thermal Cam revealed two small footprints on the third step going up to the second floor. Later, while we were investigating the third floor we again heard footsteps below. No one else was in the house and when Gerry and Willy shot the Thermal Cam down to the next level — two footsteps and a small butt pint could be seen on the second step and the hallway floor. Was Sophie waiting for us? The thermal footprints quickly faded in about 30 seconds. None of us could have gotten down that flight of stairs, left a heat print and returned unnoticed to the group, in the time it took for the prints to fade. Another piece of physical evidence of the afterlife? Perhaps. We still need to do a lot more research to find all of the answers.

Speaking of research — When I have the chance to chat with former owners of a haunted house, my first question is always, "Did you have any ghost experience?" So, I could not resist asking former owner Devra Bennung if she had any ghost experiences of her own to share.

Mrs. Bennung recalled one time when her daughter was getting married. There was an old mantel clock in the dining room that had not run for years. While her daughter was getting dressed in the back apartment, the clock started to chime. It ran all day and then stopped. Devra felt this was her late husband Karl letting her know he was there for the wedding. I think I would agree with her. Spirits will come back from Heaven for special occasions like weddings, and they will sometimes let us know they are present for the event.

After we left Ludlam (Griffin?) House and headed home, I received and email from Cathy Force. The ghosts were still active. Her daughter had put her grandson's crib in the bedroom with all of the activity. To get him to go to sleep they took his teddy bear from the crib and placed it on the dresser. When the baby woke up from his nap he was

looking for his teddy bear. It was nowhere to be found. Eventually, when they moved the crib to get into one of the locked closets in the room—they found the bear carefully placed *in the closet*. The crib had been blocking the closet and there was no way to move it without waking the baby. Cathy felt this was Sophie at work once again.

A short time later, one of Cathy's close friends, JoAnn, was sleeping in the "chapel room." JoAnn was awakened from a deep sleep in the middle of the night by something sitting on the edge of the bed. She felt the bed go down and heard a voice whisper, "Shhh—let her sleep!" Luckily, Sophie has a good ghost baby sitter!

Cathy Force plans to eventually stop renting the house and live there full-time. She wants to restore the house to the original way it was. The wall murals and stenciling and the beautiful painted parlor ceiling will once again come to life. I cannot wait to see the finished product! Since the rest of Ludlam House has already come to life, it is fitting that the house—should match the ghosts!

The Carroll Villa

FABULOUS FOOD BELOW
SPIRITS HOVERING ABOVE

Historic Hotel - 19 Jackson Street

Most people who have visited Cape May have also eaten in the fabulous Mad Batter Restaurant on Jackson Street. People tend to enjoy the food and atmosphere so much they rarely look up to see they are sitting underneath one of Cape May's venerable hotels, The Carroll Villa. Cape May has many historical gems in the architecture department and the Carroll Villa is one of them—it also happens to have a ghost or two roaming about.

As I mentioned earlier, in November of 1878 the Great Fire of Cape May destroyed almost 30 acres of real estate. By the next summer almost everything had been rebuilt, and the town was ready to receive tourists, the lifeblood of Cape May.

George Hildreth had lost several properties in the fire. Jackson Street was almost entirely wiped out, and Hildreth lost his Wyoming Cottage to the blaze. Hildreth had a local builder Charles Shaw build him a new structure, completed in 1882, which he named The Carroll Villa, in honor of Charles Carroll of Maryland, the oldest living signer of the Declaration of Independence. About ten years later a second "wing" was added with smaller rooms. This wing was thought to have been originally added as servants' quarters to accommodate the large numbers of staff Victorian families traveled with in those days.

When I dined in The Mad Batter, I always sensed someone watching me from above. Looking up through the skylights, I would visually scanned the tall towers, of the hotel for signs of life—I mean death. There was a strong presence of a woman watching me. It was one of the times in Cape May I could sense someone watching me because I

The Carroll Villa as it looked around 1900, when the ghosts were people.
(Courtesy of Don Pocher)

was a medium. This woman just knew. She must have been reading my energy or my thoughts. She was not sending me anything in the form of communication. She was psychically watching me.

A few years ago, I held my first book signing at a dinner given by MAC at the Mad Batter Restaurant. I had flown Magic (my photographer Maciek Nabrdalik) in from Poland to be at the momentous event and to snap some pictures of Jackson Street for *Book 2*.

I told Magic that we should do a shot of me looking down over the street from a vantage point above. My first thought was to go up to the turret of The Inn at 22 Jackson, featured in *Book 1*, but we could not get the right shot. While I was standing up in the turret room of the Inn at 22 Jackson, I noticed The Carroll Villa had a wonderful old cupola on top. I went inside and asked Mark Kulkowitz, who now runs the Mad Batter with his wife, Pam Huber, if I could do a psychic walk-through and snap some pictures. We had finished my first book signing at The Mad Batter below, so Mark and the staff were eagerly awaiting my paranormal report for their own Jackson Street dwelling.

The Carroll Villa has always been a hotel since it was built. Today, it is a 22 room Bed & Breakfast Hotel, with the Mad Batter Restaurant downstairs. The Kulkowitz Cape May history begins in 1974 when Harry Kulkowitz first saw the Carroll Villa while playing poker there with the current owner. Harry recognized the potential for a marvelous restaurant in the old hotel. I think he also felt some of the great energy Jackson Street had to offer. Previous to moving to Cape May, Harry had owned and operated a fine arts gallery in Philadelphia, the Kenmore Art Gallery. Harry felt that the site of the Carroll Villa triggered his creative spirits and tapped into a dream from childhood to create a special restaurant. Previously the Carroll Villa had been serving family style meals to the guests of the hotel. What Harry saw was the big empty porch, and he envisioned it covered with tables and people eating wonderful food. The only problem was that the sun would make it very uncomfortable—an awning was needed. But exterior changes to a historic building in Cape May can only be made with historic precedence. Enter Olga Thoden, with a picture of the Carroll Villa from the beginning of the century, showing the porch sporting awnings. And so was born a new restaurant—The Mad Batter.

I think all creative energy is channeled, and I do not think it was a coincidence that Harry Kulkowitz, now retired, was drawn to Jackson Street. I talk about the Jackson Street vortex in *Book 2*. Yes, the street has more hauntings (along with Columbia Avenue) then other places in town, but it is the great energy here that I was speaking of when I wrote about a vortex. Jackson Street has "Sedona, Arizona-like" energy that nourishes the soul and opens up one's energy flow to allow the higher energies to come through. I think Cape May in general has this same type of energy and that is why people love it so much—the beaches aren't bad either.

I would imagine that Harry, as a lover of art, may have also felt the creative energies flowing when he got to Cape May—and I am glad he did, and that he decided to restore this magnificent old building.

After we got the OK from Harry's son Mark, we made our way up the winding stairways of the hotel. There are two separate buildings here. One side, it was thought, was originally for guests and the other side housed the servants that came along with families in those days, much like a family today will bring along a nanny to watch the kids.

I felt two different energies in each wing. The north wing, farther away from the beach, gave me the feeling that a woman was lurking about. She felt as if she could change rooms and floors in the blink of an eye. I would come in one door and she would be gone through another, unseen, door. I later found out when the Kulkowitz family did their years of renovations, rooms were enlarged and doors were rearranged or removed. The original rooms were very small and oddly arranged, and they needed to be expanded to meet the needs of today's tourists. This woman, whoever she was, knew the old routes and still followed them, even though they were long changed.

The south wing had different energy, that of an older man. "Could this be George Hildreth?" I thought to myself. His wife Beatrice (Beaty) was haunting their old beach house (now Poor Richard's Inn) next door. Maybe he was hanging around as well?

I slowly made my way up the winding and narrow wooden steps to the building's cupola. There are several cupolas in town and I think this one and the one atop the Chalfonte are my two favorites.

The ocean breeze blew around me as I peered out of the cupola window and gazed out over Jackson Street. The energy up there was amazing.

"Let me get a shot of you looking out the window," Magic said to me as he opened another window and climbed out onto the roof.

"What are you doing?" I yelled to him, as he rekindled my dormant fear of heights and falling. My words fell on deaf ears, before I could yell, "come back in here" he moved out onto the roof top and started snapping pictures. Being the perfectionist he is, he kept mov-

ing back further and further toward the roof's edge. Imagine trying to maintain a cool and composed look as mental images of your photographer falling off a three story roof go rushing through your head! Luckily, he got the right shots and even though it appears in *Book 2*, I am running it again on the previous page in honor of Magic's bravery. Jackson Street did *not* need another ghost!

That November, MAC had asked me to do a new lecture featuring the ghosts of Christmas Past. The topic was ghostly characters that appeared (or disappeared) in Victorian literature. November and December is a busy time for me, and I was only able to be in Cape May the Friday night of the lecture. The event was to be held at The Mad Batter, and this time we would be staying there!

Willy and I raced down the Garden State Parkway and made our way through several traffic jams to get to the hotel at 7 PM. My dinner lecture was to begin at seven thirty and we were running out of time. Grabbing the luggage, the man at the front desk showed me to our room, upon the third floor. Why is the room always SO far away when one is in a rush? I sprinted up the stairs—only stopping to pop a Lipitor® so I would not be the next ghost of the hotel—arriving at our room, luggage in tow and out of breath.

Willy was parking the car, and I had about ten minutes to freshen up before the lecture. As I brushed my teeth in the bathroom, I heard Willy enter the room. I called to him, but he did not respond. Trying not to swallow my mouth full of toothpaste, I walked out of the bathroom and did a visual sweep of the bedroom area. Nothing. "Maybe another guest checking in next door," I thought and went back to getting ready.

Later that night after the lecture, Willy and I returned to our room. We were both exhausted. Between the cold, damp November weather and stairs that only Richard Simmons would love, we were ready for a good night's sleep.

I have to say, the Carroll Villa Rooms are really beautiful and this third floor room had a great view of the ocean. We both quickly fell sound asleep. At some point around 2 PM I awoke to the sound of a door opening and closing nearby. I also thought I heard someone calling me, but I could have been in a dream state when that happened.

As I mentioned in the previous books, when I am *awake* I love to investigate for ghosts. When I am asleep, I am not up for that challenge. Now, sleeping in a haunted place does present those challenges, but I am only human. I need my sleep. So after hearing the voice calling my name, I propped myself up, looked around, and when all was clear I fell back asleep.

That's when the cover started to pull off my feet.

I thought it was getting cold in the room because of the wind blowing outside. I wondered why the covers were off my feet, but figured I had pulled them off the bed in my sleep. I rolled over on my side and glanced at the mirror above the dresser. I blinked once to clear my vision, but the image was still there. There was a woman in my mirror!

"Oh crap!" I quietly exclaimed aloud as my eyes opened wide, but the rest of me froze in place. It was not a matter of being scared—I was—it

The antique dresser mirror where the phantom woman appeared to Craig.

was about not scaring away the ghost. I watched her and she was staring right back at me. A cold chill ran through my entire body as my adrenalin kicked in, to help me think of exactly how I should handle this situation. Do I bolt out of bed and grab the recorder on the dresser—which happened to be *such* a bad place for it at the moment.

In the time it took me to think the matter through, I watched her image fully form. I could see a young woman, maybe in her twenties, from her head down to her stomach. She had long, dark hair that appeared tangled. Mind you, this was all taking place in a room lit only by the moonlight and street lights below, so it was difficult to see too much detail.

There was no communication coming from her other than she was very lonely. I kept eye contact as long as I could, until she started fading into the shadows again. As she slowly disappeared, Willy woke up sensing something was wrong. I quickly sent him back under his pile of pillows when I told him what was across from us in the mirror.

As she faded, the woman reached with her right hand and combed her fingers through her hair. For a split second I saw tangles of seaweed and shells in her hair. I am not sure if this image was part psychic or all psychic. Once I saw the seaweed, I knew she had drowned. Her gray, melting form began to merge with the shadows of the room. Finally all that remained of the specter was a mental impression she left for me. I could see the shadows of furniture in the room reflecting in the mirror, but the presence had vanished. She did not return that night.

The next morning I was heading down to breakfast when I encountered a young man in his early twenties with red hair staring at the wall, in the second floor hallway of the north wing. I glanced to the wall, thinking he was checking out a picture or some other wall hanging, but it was just a section of wall paper. I turned and rounded the corner to continue on my way when I heard him say, "Good morning, Mr. McManus."

I thought he was someone who attended my lecture the previous night. I stopped, and walked around the corner to return the greeting — except he was gone. I did not hear a door open or close, and he had not been standing in a doorway when I saw him. I had not turned but a second when he spoke and was back in position in another few seconds. He would have had to have sprinted to a door, opened the door, closed it again — quietly — to vanish without me seeing or hearing him go. The man appeared to me to be perfectly human, solid and real. He was not transparent, wispy or apparition-like at all. If he had not called me by name, I would say he was just an imprint, a residual haunting, not a real ghost, but he interacted with me — or at least with my mind.

After breakfast, I took a few minutes to walk the hotel once more, both the north and south wings. While the energy in the north wing where we had spent the night, was now minimal, I found the energy of the south wing to be hopping! I stopped near the door to the stairway that leads up to the cupola and sensed "people" moving around the hallways. At one particular spot, I was drawn to an old Victorian couch sitting beneath a sunny window at the end of the hallway. I focused my energy on the piece of furniture as it was radiating a certain "extra heaviness" in my mind. This feeling is what I experience when I encounter a ghost. I can't see it, but I can feel it with my mind.

*Beware the ghostly lady with the hat,
should you decide to sit in her favorite spot!*

    The image that came into my mind was a woman with a large, festive hat sitting in the center of the couch holding the hand of a young girl seated on the couch next to her. A perfectly normal image—if they weren't both dead. These ghosts were not frightening, they were, instead, vacationing. At least that is what they were telling me.

    As I have been saying, we do not have any idea how the ghost realm works. It could be a normal stepping stone on a soul's route to Heaven. Maybe it is like a waiting room to get into Heaven and everyone there has to wait until their number is called. We just don't know how it works.

    Some ghosts are stuck and want to leave, some ghosts are stuck because they do not want to go and others are—on vacation. Go figure.

    This hotel has great energy and old world charm. I highly recommend a stay there—hoping that you will also be kind enough to keep me apprised of any further ghost sightings, should I have missed anyone! Cape May is a very special place—as is the wonderful and historic Carroll Villa.

The Virginia Hotel

YES, VIRGINIA—THERE IS A GHOST

Historic Hotel — 25 Jackson Street

ONE of my favorite haunts in all of Cape May is The Virginia Hotel — and the ghosts have nothing to do with it. The Virginia is one of the top nightspots in Cape May. At the Ebbitt Room, you will be wined and dined with dazzling dishes and a fabulous wine list. In the lounge you will be treated to fireside live music in the winter, and cool, refreshing cocktails in the summer with your choice of indoor seating or great people watching on the front veranda. It is a perfect setting for a wonderful evening in town — and it also happens to be haunted.

I have been going to The Virginia for cocktails and dinner for years now. Steve LaManna, the Virginia's former piano player, would often chat with me during and between songs. One evening, Steve and I got on the subject of ghosts and he told me about his own experience with the hotel's unseen guests.

Steve always played his grand piano facing the restaurant's glass French doors. One night, as he played through his familiar repertoire, something caught his eye. The long, brass handle of the door slowly moved down into the open position. As he looked to see who was on the other side of the door, he realized the handle was moving by itself. The door slowly opened — and then closed again. Being made of glass the doors are completely see-through. No one was on either side.

Staying at The Virginia is one of the most comfortable night's sleep one can get in town. The rooms are beautifully modernized almost to the detriment of my ghost investigating. There is so much "new" energy, it is sometimes hard to get through to the old energy! This historic hotel that was brought back from the brink of demolition by the

Bashaw family in the late 1980s. The building had been condemned after years of neglect, and the roof was about to cave in, when Keith Bashaw and his son Curtis with their Chamberlain Hospitality Group rushed to The Virginia's aid and completely restored the building to its former Victorian grandeur. The Bashaws still run The Virginia today.

Before the Bashaw's reign at The Virginia there were many different owners of the hotel. Even Henry Macomber was involved running the hotel for a time in the 1930s. In the old days, this continuous shuffling of ownership was not uncommon in town. One of these shuffles left a few stray cards on the floor in the form of ghostly energy, and I think the McConnells are at the heart of the haunting here.

Alexander W. McConnell owned several properties on this side of Jackson Street before the Great Fire of 1878, including the St. Elmo Hotel. McConnell is listed in the 1874 Cape May city directory as hav-

Above: An early postcard showing The Ebbitt around 1905 before it was renamed The Virginia. (Courtesy of Walt Campbell)

ing a cottage at 53 Jackson Street. The word "cottage" implied it was not a permanent residence, it was a summer house. Once the fire was finished with the area, McConnell had to rebuild and he erected his new hotel, then called The Ebbitt House, in 1883 on his property on the east side of Jackson Street.

Either his son or his brother, John McConnell, took charge of the hotel and was listed as the Manager of The Ebbitt House in the 1907 Cape May city directory. Then he disappears from town. Another postcard I have in my collection shows The Ebbitt under new ownership, with a new name, The Virginia. Samuel Ludlam's son A. Marcy, and his ex-wife Elmira, were running the hotel in 1910. After that time, the McConnells vanished from Cape May history from that point onward.

When I investigated Congress Hall in the summer of 2000 with General Manager Patrick Logue, I was shown two large portraits that dated from the Victorian era. Patrick Logue said they were discovered in the basement of The Virginia during renovation. The management and he were under the assumption that the portraits depicted Alfred and Ellen Ebbitt, the first owners of the Ebbitt House.

"No," I told Patrick, "Those names are not resonating with me at all." I felt the pictures were of someone else. Today I feel the stately looking couple in the portraits may be Mr. & Mrs. Alexander McConnell, the people who *really* built the hotel. I believe The Ebbitt House was named for its larger namesake that sat at 14th Street and F Avenue in Washington D.C. in the late 1800s. This was a hotel that many of the businessmen in Cape May knew well. People like Henry Sawyer and Dr. Samuel Ware had businesses near the hotel. It would be appropriate to name a new hotel in a resort so close to Washington D.C. after a famous hotel in that city.

I have encountered both the ghost of a man and a woman in the downstairs lounge, especially the north porch. The third floor is also a hot spot of activity and several people have told me that they stayed

The McConnells or the Ebbitts? Even their ghosts won't tell us.

there and had experienced "something" paranormal. I had my own experience in one of the upper rooms.

It was a few years ago when Willy and I stayed at The Virginia for the very first time. I remember thinking how plush and comfortable the bed was and how "new" the room energy felt. I did not have a feeling of sleeping in a 120-year-old building at all.

We drifted off to sleep and somewhere around 3:30 AM, I got up to get a glass of water. I was not sure why I woke up — maybe it was the four glasses of wine I had before I went to bed. As I made my way to the bathroom I heard someone knocking on another door in the hallway. Being the nosy body I am, I quietly put my ear to the room door and listened. I was more interested to hear who would be knocking at a hotel room door so early in the morning. I heard no response.

As I started back to bed, the knocking came again, this time closer to *my* room! This was my cue to turn on the ghost hunting circuit in my brain. I quickly opened the door and looked down the hall. Nothing. Not a creature was stirring, not even a ghost.

The knocking stopped at that point and since no one else opened their doors. Either the floor was occupied by sound sleepers or I was hearing the sound psychically.

Compared to other places on Jackson Street, the ghosts here are usually subdued. I have felt the ghost of a woman sit next to me on the couch in the bar on several occasions. From what I felt, she was at one time a hostess or proprietress of the hotel. She felt like she was there to keep things running smoothly and at The Virginia, things are kept at a very professional level. This woman did not have as old a feeling about her as the ghosts of the McConnells had. She felt younger, more recent. She also felt like she did not have a family.

In the late Robert Magee's book, *Vintage Cape May*, Magee gives his account of The Ebbitt/Virginia history and mentions that during World War I, the hotel was used as a social club, for Navy men stationed in Cape May. He also goes on to note that in 1924 The Virginia was sold to Dr. W. S. Hoffman of Philadelphia, and that an announcement in the local paper two weeks later says that the doctor was going to change the hotel into a sanitarium for diabetics, which apparently never happened. I wondered why I keep craving The Ebbitt Room's Sticky Toffee Pudding!

I have been talking with several friends who grew up in Cape May and have questioned them about the history of The Virginia. They all had interesting stories to tell, but one of the most unique apparently happened sometime in the 1930s, when a local resident who owned the hotel was caught by his wife having an affair. When he returned home that night, she had taken all the money and her belongings and left the house. When the man died, his wife, expecting to inherit the hotel, was shocked to find out that he left it to his mistress! Could this be the lonely lady hostess?

Sometimes ghosts just don't have a sense of humors. When I arrived at The Virginia one evening, the staff had been talking about the huge commotion that happened the week before. It seems the huge portrait of "Mrs. McConnell" on the wall had become unanchored and crashed to the floor. Luckily the ornate Victorian frame only needed minor repair. About this same time, several members of the staff were joking that, Mrs. McConnell, looked more like a "Mr." McConnell. I warned them that she could hear what they were saying, but no one listened. At least, Mrs. McConnell didn't lift herself off the wall and crown someone over the head with her picture, like Captain Gregg in *The Ghost and Mrs. Muir.*

I wonder, when a building falls into neglect like The Virginia did years ago, what the ghosts actually see. Did they see the hotel the way it originally was? Did they notice the run down state of the property back in the sixties and seventies? Do they see all of the changes done by the current owners? Part of me thinks they enjoyed the place being closed. We, the living, were not around to annoy them. On the other hand, some ghosts seem to enjoy contact with the living, while others avoid the living at all costs. The activity here has been sensed by others on the third floor.

Ghosts will move away from us, as far as they can go and that usually means moving to a forgotten spot on some higher floor. They love attics because humans rarely go there. Do the ghosts at The Virginia come and go? Since this has always been a hotel are the ghosts here transient? Do they travel to Cape May, stay at a former lodging place and then return to their homes?

From what I have captured on tape, the ghosts seem to be talking about day to day activities like eating or cleaning. Do they exist in a world like ours except their physical matter is in the form of pure energy that only they can see and interact with? Will we all see this "new horizon" when we die, and leave our bodies behind? I guess we will only find out when we get there. Maybe Cape May is a vacation spot for people in Heaven as well. Wouldn't that be something.

To be on the safe side, I always recommend toasting the McConnells, or whoever is in the portraits on the wall at The Virginia. You can never tell when a ghost will be listening — or decide to *drop in.*

Ghosts of the West

A JOURNEY INTO WEST CAPE MAY...
SOME OF THE OLDEST HAUNTS IN TOWN

West Cape May

WEST Cape May is often overlooked by travellers, coming into town on vacation. For history buffs, this is the place to go as some of these houses date back to Colonial days. In regard to ghosts and hauntings, the older the dwelling and the more history it has, the better the chance of finding a ghost.

The Borough of West Cape May was originally known as Eldredge, named for the family who settled here in the early 1800s and added generations of children to the population. The original land belonged to Native Americans who sold a large tract to a man named Joseph Whilldin. Whilldin and others bartered with early Native Americans, to buy tracts of land, in and around Cape May. Whilldin's two sons, Isaac and Joseph, Jr., inherited their father's lands and when the sons finally died, their grandchildren began to sell the lands outside of the family.

In 1884, the Borough of West Cape May was incorporated and today this wonderful, bucolic hamlet to the west of Cape May City holds a mix of residential properties, Bed & Breakfasts and Inns and farmland and vineyards. It also has its share of ghostly citizens, many of whom have been haunting here for over 100 years.

Sometimes I think I am doing such a wonderful thing by writing about these forgotten specters. Yet, at other times, I think the ghosts must simply hate me! I keep revealing their last hiding spots and disturbing their solitude by sending droves of ghost loving humans their way. No wonder I keep getting told to "f--- off!" on my EVP tapes! I wonder if this means I lose my eternal ocean front rights when I die?

An old postcard from the beginning of the last century shows Wilberham (Wilbraham) Park as it was in John Wilbraham's day. Didn't anyone ever spellcheck in those days? (Courtesy of Walt Campbell)

Anyway, West Cape May is such a cool place because every building that I have investigated has this long, magical history. More than once, I have found myself daydreaming, about the old days in Cape May. The time when whaling families first arrived from Long Island or Massachusetts, to settle on the bay at what was then called, "Town Bank" or "New England Town." As those bluff top settlements started to erode into the sea, the founding families moved inland and settled the rest of the peninsula.

Historians Joan Berkey and Mike Conley have just finished a magnificent 700 page historical survey of West Cape May that is on display at the Borough Hall on Broadway. The study reveals that Cape May has even more historical architectural gems than once thought, and now there is finally a historical preservation ordinance in West Cape May. These old homes and buildings (and ghosts) will be preserved for generations to come.

My first foray into West Cape May was a visit to Daniel's Restaurant on Broadway. It is currently operating as the Moonfish Grill. The house is historically called The Whilldin–Miller House and was once the home of Joseph Whilldin. The rear section of the house is thought pre-date 1730, being one of the oldest structures in town. The newer front section of the house (see picture to the right) was added on by Jonas Miller when he was fixing the house up for his daughter in the 1860s. It is currently haunted by a ghost named Catherine and an unnamed soldier, thought to be a left over of the French-Indian war.

This house has a long history of being haunted and as good as the food is, I go primarily for the ghosts! To read the entire story, on the Whilldin–Miller House, check out the chapter on this house in, *The Ghosts of Cape May Book 1*.

It was this house that reminded me that Cape May does not end at the city limits. There is much more to see to the west. The Albert Stevens Inn and The Wilbraham Mansion were, in my mind, "West Cape May." I had never bothered to go any further in my mind. If it was not near Daniel's or CVS on Myrtle Avenue, I did not know about it. What I was missing!

Over the years, I became friends with several people in West Cape May, and they always lamented being overlooked by the powers that be in the tourism promoting industry. Even when I first started doing our Ghost Trolley Tours with MAC, we did not have the available trolleys or manpower to get a tour routed through West Cape May. It was not until I pitched the idea of adding a new tour to the lighthouse and having the trolley pass through West Cape May did we venture west.

Jimmy Labrusciano, co-owner of The Albert Stevens Inn, was instrumental in rounding up other haunted property owners to be part of the new tour. Jimmy came up with a list and phone numbers and I went to work doing some surface investigations. Unfortunately, not all of the places people thought were haunted had ghosts. Sometimes it was a loose window or settling joists causing the "haunting." There were a handful of legitimate haunted houses in the mix however, and you will read about them in the following pages.

The enchanted Whilldin-Miller House — presently incarnated as The Moonfish Grill

Historic dwellings, need constant upkeep and usually have to undergo a series of upgrades, expansions or changes over time. In West Cape May, many of these old building were also moved to their current location from somewhere else on the peninsula. The house next to the Albert Stevens Inn, was moved from Cape May Point. Eldredge House was moved from Jackson Street over 150 years ago to its present location on Broadway. Moving and changing a home will definitely shake up the energy in a building, but it will rarely shake the ghosts. Move a house, the ghosts go along for the ride. Hey, if someone took your house away, wouldn't you follow it?

I have added enough history to give you a good idea about who is haunting, but I have certainly not covered all the history there is, that would be a whole other book in itself! If you want more history and want to see most of these houses, I highly recommend you take our, *Ghosts of the Lighthouse* trolley tour which will take you past many of these haunts. In the meantime, let's take a short trip out of Cape May and enjoy a leisurely, haunted stroll through *the other* Cape May.

The Albert Stevens Inn
A FOLLOW UP VISIT TO THE DOCTOR
B&B 127 Myrtle Avenue — West Cape May

I KNEW there were ghosts in the house. I could feel them as I entered the front door. One of them was a very commanding presence, that of someone watching over the house. The energy permeated every room and every corridor. As I looked for the ghosts, it was clear that the ghosts, were also looking for me — they also knew exactly what I was doing there and why I had come.

The Doctor was *in*.

One of the best opportunities for me to stick my psychic nose inside of potential new Cape May haunts was by taking MAC's historic house tours each fall. There is always something or someone new to see inside these great old places. Sometimes I sense something, other times there is nothing. Not every house in Cape May is haunted — one or two don't have ghosts.

At the Albert Stevens Inn, the doctor was definitely *in* on the day I paid my visit. The ghost in question is Dr. Albert Gateton Stevens (1870-1942) and he may have been dead for more than 60 years, but that doesn't stop him from watching over everyone, and everything, that comes and goes in his old home. The Albert Stevens Inn is one of Cape May's most delightful Victorian B&Bs.

When I first met Albert Stevens co-owner, Lenanne Labrusciano, I could sense she was an old soul who was in touch with the energy of the house. Old souls are those people who have reincarnated many times and have gathered lots of life experience and wisdom. When I encounter old souls, there is a certain feel about them. There is something about their energies that just radiates. I think Cape May, with its relaxing setting by the sea and its historical setting, attracts certain old souls to settle down there. I hope to be one of those old souls settling in Cape May one day.

After introducing myself as a psychic medium on the MAC historic house tour, Lenanne told me that they have indeed had guests report activity in the old Victorian home. I spent a few minutes in the front parlor area where I felt the energy at the time to be the strongest. I could hear, in my head, a man's deep, commanding voice telling me he was the previous owner of the home. It was Dr. Stevens.

Lenanne had asked me to go upstairs and see if I could find where all the activity on the second floor was happening. I found a rear bedroom, formerly Dr. Stevens' reading room, to be the hot spot. I found the ghost of an older woman, who did not (or chose not to) identify herself. This room, confirmed Lenanne, was where several guests reported doors opening and closing and the bed shaking.

Okay I thought, doors open, close, the bed shakes, it's just another "garden variety" haunting. I made a mental note of it and returned to the living downstairs. On leaving, I told Lenanne that her ghosts were sending her a warning about a problem in the cellar. Some appliance or something was about to break and cause trouble. She mentioned they would check the furnace. We said our good-byes and parted.

About a year later, I began writing my *Ghost Writer* column in *Exit Zero*. I kept thinking back to the previous October, about Dr. Stevens and the house, and wondering what the old boy may have been up to in my absence. I gave Lenanne a call, and she agreed to be a part of my ghostly journal of Cape May.

On a muggy day during the following summer, I returned to the Albert Stevens Inn. In between checking in guests, Lenanne graciously spent some time with me as we further unraveled the mystery of the old house.

The first thing Lenanne had to tell me about was the ghost's prediction from last fall. "My cousin Chris, was watching the house for us in November. In the middle of the night, he just got a weird feeling that woke him up. He had this odd sensation that something was wrong and went downstairs to find the basement flooded... the sump

pump had burned out!" When ghosts mention a problem in the place where they reside—listen! I have been presented with this type of information before and it can be very valuable to a homeowner to hear what their ghosts are warning them about.

At this point, I felt a quick *swish* of cold air pass me. This is one way I sense a ghost. Some people think the cold breezes or rushes of air (natural causes ruled out) are caused by a flow of negative ions, the type that home air purifiers give off. This feels cool and refreshing to the skin. Ghosts may also use negative ionic charges of energy to exist on this plane. When ghosts move by us, we feel a cold spot or rush of cool air. The charge from negative ions can also cause the hair on our arms and neck to stand up.

This is only one theory of cold spots. Another theory proposes that ghosts may actually be drawing energy from us. Using us as some sort of fuel to manifest and get up the energy to communicate or move closer to us. When their plane and our plane of existence touch, the meeting causes some sort of exchange of energy, and we experience this exchange as a cold sensation. These are all theories for the moment. One thing is certain—cold spots on a hot day (natural and artificial causes excluded) can be a calling card for a ghost.

Paranormal researchers will only accept cold spots as evidence of a ghost being present, when there is a significant temperature drop of more than 10 degrees in a short time. I have felt cold spots materialize out of nowhere and actually circle around a room (and me) and then vanish with no natural explanation.

I get a certain psychic feeling in these situations, that feeling, when coupled with dropping temperature, becomes a good enough barometer for me to use as an indicator of ghost activity nearby. Cold spots in a haunting are some form of energy exchange. We just can't say for sure what is happening. Science has yet to tell us. For me, unexplainable cold spots are like a sign post reading "ghost ahead."

Pictured left—the late and not-so-late Dr. Albert Stevens.
Can you read this entire page without noticing that he's watching you?

I did a basic walk around on the first floor of the Inn with Lenanne. I felt a particularly strong energy in and around the dining room. As I moved through the room, I could see in my mind's eye two women wearing white, one older, one younger. They were hovering over the table. They were not serving food or eating, but staring down at the something I could not see. I got the names, "Tessie" and "Bessie," or "Vessie" and "Bessie."

"Bessie, was Dr. Stevens' wife, and Vesta was his daughter, who lived here until 1980," Lenanne told me.

"Why are they hovering over this table?" I asked Lenanne. They appeared to still be looking at something.

"This was Dr. Stevens' examining room," Lenanne informed me.

Yes, I thought, that's why they were wearing white, but what were they examining? Before I could get an answer to that question from the women, the ghost of a young boy, sprung into my psychic sight, from on top of the table and bolted out the door! I had not seen him there until he made his hasty exit. I sensed that he had died of some tonsil or throat problem. He ran out the side door and vanished.

Had I uncovered a doctor's office for ghosts? I wonder if they accept *Boo Cross and Boo Shield?*

I later discovered that Dr. Albert Stevens was known in his day as a "homeopathic" doctor who created his own medicines and cures in a laboratory in the room above his back doctor's office. This encounter made me think the Stevens crew were some sort of Spirit Guides who have returned to help the ghosts—some form of missionaries. We do it, why wouldn't higher beings?

The Stevens family, is an old-time clan in town, with roots going way back. Like the Eldredges, the Reeves and many other old names in West Cape May, there are many Stevens family members in West Cape May's history. Was the doctor acting alone or were there other of his relatives hanging out in town?

So many ghosts are related to each other in Cape May. I know they talk, so one of them must have started this mass haunting thing.

Somebody knows a secret about the afterlife and Cape May!

The dining room—formerly Dr. Stevens' examining room

Lenanne has also had a first-hand encounter with her ghosts. One day, after they first took over the Inn and were doing major restoration work, she was painting an upstairs bedroom. Her dog was with her in the back upstairs bedroom, the same room in which I had felt the presence. As she recalled, "He (the dog) kept looking at me. He got up, started growling, and I told him to come lay down. He heard something in the room. I said, 'It's okay, just lay down.' A few minutes later he got up again, went to the doorway and started growling again at the empty hallway, and the hair came up on his back. He was scared. I thought I heard a voice also, and I thought, 'Okay, that's it, and got down off the ladder and went downstairs!"

Animals can and do sense ghosts. Cats are especially sensitive to the paranormal and many feel they can actually see the ghosts. Dogs also react to ghostly energy, although not in the same way as cats will react. Cats will sit and watch — dogs will typically growl and run.

"I have had previous guests who have said that they have felt that someone was up in that room." The room in question is Dr. Stevens' reading room, and was originally part of his bedroom. It would make sense that a strong presence like Dr. Stevens would be felt in his private domain. By strong, I do not mean negative, I mean a strong personality, like a person who can walk into a room and command the attention of all present.

I felt the doctor's presence more in the front of the house, in the parlor. It seems that the whole family comes and goes.

"The doctor passed in 1942, and Bessie, his wife, passed in 1945. Vesta took care of her parents as they got older," Lenanne told me.

I tried to run a cassette tape in the parlor and invite the ghosts, especially the doctor, to speak to me on the tape. If they were this strong in energy, they may be able to give me a few good EVPs. One theory is that EVPs are recorded on tape telekinetically through thought energy. My brain was definitely picking up strong psychic energy, so I thought I would have a good chance to record a few words. The family chose silence, at least I heard nothing when I played the tape back on the recorder. Unfortunately, doing this I missed out on all of the quieter, Class B & C EVPs that were embedded in the white noise of the recording. Once I had uploaded the recording onto my computer, I was able to pick out a few EVPs.

The first EVP voice I recorded was rather amusing. I ask if there is anyone here and a woman's voice says, "There's no one here."

I ask again if there is anyone here and a man says, "We're here." It's great to get a direct response to a question. The problem is having to wait to upload the recording to hear the response.

In another EVP, a man says, "Let her join," followed by a woman clearly saying, "Albert."

Two men spoke on the tape. One was talking about a medical problem and the other seemed to be asking him questions. Another man says, "Get into quarantine." Hearing this confirmed my suspicion that

The Doctor is definitely — IN

Dr. Stevens has not yet fully retired. I have encountered other ghostly doctors in Cape May and now I am certain they are all still working! Let's face it, we do not know what is going on in the *ghost realm* or on the Other Side in Heaven, for that matter. Even disembodied souls may care. When I mention encountering a ghost in a back bedroom, a man's voice says, "Bedroom." This voice sounded like a man about Dr. Stevens' age when he died.

A few women's voices were also on the tape at various times while I was interviewing Lenanne. Most of the voices were faint and in the background and because it was August, I could not rule out that the tape recorded some street noises. I took the most realistic sounding, clearest voices as true EVPs.

The ghosts had now moved to the back of the house, into the old office. At this point in an investigation, when I start to peel away the layers of camouflaged energy, looking deeper than what we see in our reality, I may start to encounter other entities.

"I am getting the name 'Jackie' or 'Jack' or something like that," I told Lenanne, as she laughed in recognition of the name.

"You know why?" she asked us. "Vesta had a boyfriend after her husband had passed away, and he lived here in this part of the house. His name was Jack Claypool. He was a lifetime resident in Cape May, and his mother was a school teacher in town."

Hmmm — Could Vesta's second love still be hanging around?

"When Vesta died, he was the executor of the will. She left half of everything to him and the rest got split between eight cousins," Lenanne recounted.

After Lenanne and Jim had bought the house, a neighbor had told Lenanne, that it was too bad that Jack had just died, as he would have loved to had told them about the house. Well, it was not too late. It seems old Jack is still "hanging" with the Stevens!

I invited Jack Claypool to speak on tape from the Other Side, but he chose to take the "fifth" also, not uttering an audible word. I cannot say whether it is possible or not for all ghosts to leave EVPs. They seem to show up when you least expect it. Maybe they cannot physically hide from a psychic medium, but they can choose to be silent. This may be their way of politely asking to be left alone.

At a point in our visit to the back part of the Albert Stevens Inn, the old side door of the Doctor's office opened and closed. A patient arriving, I wondered?

Lenanne mentioned to me that the day was full of strange happenings. "I had some weird things happen today. I was folding clothes, and I put my tea towels up on a shelf on top of the dryer where I put folded washcloths. All of a sudden, the tea towels came down and hit me in the head. I folded them again, put them up on the shelf again, and they came right back down and hit me on the head!"

"Somebody was playing with you," I told Lenanne.

"That's the impression I got," adding, "then the wash cloths came down and hit me in the head! I was like, 'What's going on?'"

John R. (Jack) Claypool, died on Christmas Day in 1998. He and his mother Emily were neighbors of the Stevens for many years. Jack Claypool may still be hanging around the place, or he may come and go from his old home to the Albert Stevens Inn.

Jack told us that he and Vesta were still in the house. He also mentioned that Dr. and Mrs. Stevens come and go as they like. Dr. Stevens has already been back to the Other Side and returns with his wife to try to convince Vesta to cross over with them. Vesta enjoys life right where she is and she indicated to me, via Jack, that she does not want to see her old husband on the Other Side when she crosses over — as she prefers Jack now! Such a soap opera! Can you imagine a soap announcer saying, "These are the *Days of Our Deaths...*"

Vesta and Jack had originally planned to move on. Vesta had waited around as Jack grew older. She was almost twenty years his senior. When Jack died, they stayed just a little while longer to watch what would happen to their precious home. The home meant a lot to the Stevens family. It had been commissioned as a wedding present from Dr. Stevens to his bride, Bessie, in 1892 when the property was purchased from the Wilbrahams next door.

This beautiful, Queen-Anne-style home was sold to investors upon the death of Vesta Stevens-Olsen. Happily, the Labruscianos have restored the house to its former beauty, and luckily (for us) it is now a wonderful Bed and Breakfast for all to enjoy!

I will also put it on record that Lenanne serves *the most delicious breakfast in town!* There are many other great breakfasts served, but in my opinion hers is on top of the list. Don't hate me, everyone else.

That day, during the initial investigation, the light in the hall began to flicker behind Lenanne. I sensed the presence of Dr. Stevens again. He wanted to talk about the war years. He was worried about the U-boats during World War II and that the Germans would come on to the peninsula and take over. He said he took the precaution of hiding some money in a wall of the house! He would not tell us where. Maybe he was just teasing us.

150   The Albert Stevens Inn

It was not without just cause that the Doctor should worry about intruders. In his lifetime as a practicing physician, he had some "locals" break in, looking for drugs in his office. He took to making sure things were well hidden in the house.

Bringing up the incident with the sump pump, Jack took credit for waking up Lenanne's cousin Chris, in the middle of the night that November. Jack also mentioned telling Lenanne about a side door that was not locking correctly. At the time they bought the house, they did not know the door did indeed have an old-fashioned lock, so they left it unlocked. A previous guest who was clairvoyant came to Lenanne a few years ago and told her about the spirit telling him to tell Lenanne to fix the door lock!

The ghosts mentioned other children being in the house. However, Vesta was the only child. Was Dr. Stevens also a pediatrician? There certainly was a lot of movement in the house. I explained to Lenanne that a person will not usually "see" a physical form of a ghost. What one experiences in a "haunted" house is a feeling of not being alone.

Occasionally you may catch a glimpse of "something." But you will not see any headless servants or dead Irish maids, invisible from the waste down, floating toward you with a tray of scones. No chain rattling or sheet-covered ghouls—just some occasional blurs of light or shadows caught out of the corner of your eye, or maybe even, if you are lucky and intuitive, a fast glimpse of a human figure. Ghosts can be "sensed" by the living, sometimes heard, but seldom seen.

"I get that a lot!" said Lenanne. "I'll see things—I see that (the blurs and shadows) upstairs a lot," she added.

I sensed at one point, what I thought was music playing throughout the house.

"Vesta was noted as being a beautiful singer who played the piano, people told me they would come here to sing and listen to her play," Lenanne mentioned.

Throughout the investigation, I kept glancing out the window, to the Wilbraham Mansion next door. Each time I would look over at the windows of the old house I would sense a ghostly woman staring back at me. I felt she could hear everything I was saying about the house. Could ghosts have super-hearing in the form of telepathic eavesdropping? She would have to wait, until I had time to for another investigation. (You just have to wait until the next chapter.)

I had included a chapter on The Albert Stevens Inn in the first edition of *The Ghosts of Cape May Book 1*. When I began compiling all of the West Cape May stories, I knew this chapter really belonged with all of the other West Cape haunts. So, I exhumed it from *Book 1* and bought a plot for it in the future *Book 3*.

I decided to return to the Albert Stevens Inn in April 2007, with Willy and Gerry Eisenhaur and his fiance Erin Long. Appropriately, it was Friday the 13th of April at midnight, when we decided to have our first seance in the house. Willy and I were staying in the spacious attic suite and Gerry and Erin were on the second floor in the Doctor's old lab, now a bedroom.

We decided to set up in Doctor Stevens' old bedroom to see if we could get some clear EVPs. The room felt active when I first walked in. It was that feeling of not being alone. Even though, many ghosts are active while we sleep and vice versa, something was already in the bedroom when we arrived with our equipment.

There is a theory with EVP recording that suggests adding white noise to the background of an EVP recording session. The thought is that this white noise acts as carrier waves that ghosts can manipulate and change to their own vocal signals. Some people will run a radio set between stations or an air conditioner or fan blowing on high to produce continuous white noise. We decided to try this out and set a clock radio to static between stations. It was a total disaster. The only thing on that part of the tape was white noise, and lots of it! It was a train wreck of EVP recording and not one voice could be pulled from the wreckage.

If EVPs are produced via telepathic signals, these should be a higher energy than typical sound waves. Therefore, adding more sound to the mix does not seem to be the answer. I have recorded some of my best EVPs in (excuse the pun) dead silence. So before you go running around turning on every major appliance in a haunted house, try recording solo first.

I needed to filter out hiss and noise from the session twice before I could hear any signs of EVP voices. It was like trying to listen to a conversation while standing in a tornado—I was waiting for Margaret Hamilton to come flying by on a broom.

The first batch of voices were talking about Erin. They knew her or recognized her from somewhere. As far as I knew this was Erin's first trip to Cape May, but she did fall in love with the place right away and I had a strong feeling she had spent time in some past life or past lives in town. The ghosts seemed to be confirming this.

If our appearance changes from lifetime to lifetime, our soul signature must stay constant. Ghosts exist in forms that match our base souls and must be able to recognize all living creatures on a soul level. I feel I have been in Cape May in past lives, and I have certainly recognized old souls on a psychic level many times over the years. Maybe

The ghosts took turns sitting in the antique wing-back chair next to Craig during his channeling session in Dr. Stevens' old master bedroom.

ghosts only recognize us on a soul basis and see past our own physical incarnations.

We taped another twenty minutes or so of the white noise backed session. During that time, I felt something enter the room and sit in the chair beside me. The room was completely dark with the exception of Gerry's lighted meters. I sat in one of two old Victorian chairs next to the window, near the bed. Cold air began to fill the space by the old Victorian chair next to me. An entity came into my space and wanted to communicate.

At this point, when an entity pushes my way and I am already in a relaxed state, I can easily slip into a trance. Ghosts are like my version of Nyquil®, they enter my system and all I want to do is go to sleep!

The entity coming through, identified himself as Doctor Stevens. He started to ramble about medicine and his experiments at a frantic pace. He wanted to get the information onto our tape.

Dr. Stevens talked about "mind is greater than matter," but "the mind is (made) of matter" and they must "balance each other in nature." He said it is an "eternal battle" between the two. The Doctor's voice suddenly went breathy and gasping to full-throttle.

"You have a cough my dear — can I get you some horehound drops?" He said referring to Erin's cold she was battling on the trip. "Might I recommend a tisane of Tansy — unless you are allergic to it."

The only references I could find to "tisane of Tansy," which is basically the herb Tansy steeped in hot water to make tea, was the centuries old practice of using the tisane to get rid of intestinal parasites, nothing about relieving coughs and — in large quantities Tansy tea is *toxic*. Thanks Doc. Getting lonely over there?

I *did* find Erin horehound candies at The Fudge Kitchen, and that herb *is* used to treat coughs and Erin did try them and felt much better the rest of the weekend.

The man claiming to be Dr. Stevens continued to talk to us about various energy levels he needed to pass through in order to make contact. His voice came in and out and each time he faded into a pause of silence, the EVPs in the background began in earnest.

Voices of two men and one woman could be heard. I could make out a few words here and there, but nothing of significance. They were having a conversation and it did not include us in the discussion.

One EVP stood out, while the Doctor was speaking. A clear older man's voice said, "Hear me talk." I was not sure if this was the Doctor's voice coming through on tape or if it was another male presence in the room. Could I be channeling the Doctor as he is also sending telepathic signals to the tape? What if both tape and medium are simply redundant receptors of telekinetic messages?

There were a few more "Class A" EVPs that sounded like a person was standing in the room with us, except they weren't. When I first started to focus and ask the ghosts of the house for help, a male voice says, after a few minutes of no EVPs, "Let's just cooperate."

I also got a bawdy response from one of the female ghosts that was present. I had complained that the ghosts were not being very helpful tonight. I had been trying to get them to manifest a cold spot or something in the beginning and they were not putting out. When I complained, a woman's voice says, "Up yours!" Nice. Obviously someone on the Doctor's staff has no graveside manners.

Lenanne told me that Vesta was very lady-like and proper, as was her mother. Vesta had actually won "Woman of the Year" in Cape May twice. Let's just hope that it was only a disgruntled patient coming through on the tape or perhaps she was just confused as to what field of medicine the good doctor was practicing.

Multiple entities tried coming through during my channeling session. When I listened to the tape later, I could hear them all struggling to be heard. They could apparently hear us clearly for when I asked that very question, a "nice" woman's voice replied, "I can."

In trance channeling there is always a good margin for error. Multiple energies are usually converging at once. How well the medium is focused will affect the purity of the message. With any kind of psychic communication, the human brain tends to apply the "stained glass window effect" on any information. If a message comes through from the Other Side and does not seem correct with the mind that it is being channeled, that mind may "adjust" the information to a point that it feels is now correct. I think this happens on a subconscious level, but it does happen. The most pure psychic information is the immediate thought, the information when it first arrives in the split second it enters a psychic's mind. If that information hangs around for even a few seconds more in the brain of the receiver, it has the potential to get altered.

The information, is like sunlight in its pure form. If that sunlight should pass through a stained glass window, the light is changed. It is still the same light. The light has now been altered by a filter. The human mind can be a filter, and this is the primary reason that I use trance channeling information only in certain situations. If information comes through in a channeling that feels "right" or if the information is something profound, then I will include it in the investigation.

Should the entity give some details that helped to solve a mystery in the case, I will also reveal that information, but most of the trance channeled evidence I get stays right in my audio or video files.

Many of the people who come through in trance tend to be colorful characters. Unfortunately, much of the information that comes through in trance is useless chatter, mundane conversation or information that is just too vague. I *have* channeled some very profound souls, but even their information seems to start out strong and then becomes watered down as the session continues. I am not being negative about trance channeling. I feel there should be a caveat that goes along with it. In the right setting, with the right medium, it can be a wonderful way to gather information. Trance channeled information should only be used as partial evidence, not the entire evidence.

Perhaps in channeling, only the strongest personality types can get through to a medium's mind. Whoever that man was, late that night at The Albert Steven's Inn, he seemed to know why we were there and was doing his best to help us keep the communication lines open. He also was affecting Gerry's equipment.

When Dr. Stevens came through, the ambient temperature would suddenly drop from around 72 degrees, or room temperature, down to 66 degrees. Gerry watched it happen each time the entity arrived. When the entity left, the temperature would rise back to normal.

After listening to the tape, I do believe I was channeling the real Dr. Albert Stevens. He had a strong presence and a feeling that he truly belonged in the house. When I awoke from the trance we continued to run the tape. I asked the ghosts if they had anything else to add.

In the white noise a child's voice says, "Let me through! I want to go to him! I wanna go home!"

Following that an adult voice, slightly distorted replies, "You have a good home."

I felt that a young boy's ghost sensed what I was doing and wanted to communicate with me, but the adult ghosts were holding him back. He must have wanted me to help him get back to wherever he lived when he was alive. The adult ghosts knew better.

For ghosts there are few roads back home — verbal communication through a medium being one avenue.

The Albert Stevens Inn is a wonderful Bed & Breakfast and one of the gems of Cape May. If you want a nice, quiet stay, with some of the best food in town, this is the place to stay.

If you are into the paranormal, this wonderful old house will not disappoint. The Albert Stevens Inn gives new meaning to the words, "Doctors who make house calls."

The Doctor is definitely *in*.

The Wilbraham Mansion

THE IRON MAGNATE MEETS THE GHOST MAGNET

Historic Inn

133 Myrtle Avenue — West Cape May

CAPE MAY is fortunate to have a treasure trove of wonderful old historic houses within its boundaries. Fortunately, for lovers of all things paranormal, many of them are also haunted! One of the most beautiful places to stay in town is the old Wilbraham Mansion in West Cape May. I had admired the house for many years, every time I walked through Wilbraham Park, in front of the mansion.

Today, the Wilbraham Mansion is a wonderful B&B run by Doug Carnes and his family, a place that lovers of the Victorian era will enjoy very much.

When I was investigating the Albert Stevens Inn next door, I told owners Jimmy and Lenanne Labrusciano that I was sensing ghosts in their neighbor's mansion. The Labruscianos told me that the former owner was an elderly woman who sold the place to the current owners, the Carnes family. They knew from an old deed that earlier owners of the property also sold a piece of the estate to Dr. Albert Stevens whose family then built the Labrusciano's house on the western side of the property.

I finally had the opportunity to stay at The Wilbraham in late summer of 2005. I chose the suite on the third floor of the mansion. In many old buildings the upper floor is usually the perfect place to do ghost research. This is not because the ghosts are former servants. It is because the ghosts want to get away from the living, not haunt them. Ghosts want to peacefully coexist with us and most of the time they try to stay out of our way. We are usually not as gracious.

The innkeepers had stepped out when we arrived at the mansion that summer, so we let ourselves in. The impressive building has not one, but two formal parlors. Apparently, in his day, Mr. Wilbraham was quite the entertainer — hosting parties for high profile south Jersey folks like department store magnate John Wanamaker.

Following the instructions on our welcome letter, we made our way up the winding staircases to the top floor of the house. It reminded me of an old movie I had seen in which the guests arrive at the old house, the door opens by itself, and they find their way to their rooms. I must admit, even though the door did not open by itself, I loved the idea of getting to first experience the house by myself, without a guide giving me too much background information.

After we settled down in our third floor suite, in what used to be the attic section of the mansion, I could sense the ghosts of children in the room. Two younger children, a boy and a girl had come to greet me. With them was an older woman who gave me the name "Ann." I told the children that I was there to investigate the house for ghosts and that I would be running a tape recorder later that night. The response from the ghosts was much more enthusiastic then I had imagined.

As I have mentioned previously, when I encounter a ghost, I do not see or hear them with my eyes or ears — I interact with them with my mind. Ghosts are energy fields with a brain. They can think and act, but have trouble doing anything that requires physical contact. They rarely can manifest enough energy to create a visible apparition and have great difficulty moving physical objects or creating actual sounds. Some ghosts, however, have been around long enough to outdo their peers in any of these departments.

I told the children and Ann that I would be resting for a while after the three hour car ride south, and I would conduct my investigation later that evening. I fell asleep quickly and had a great, long nap. I had very vivid dreams of people I did not know, and after awakening, wondered if when we sleep we move to a spot closer to where ghosts exist. Could I have been wandering around the ghost's realm by being

The haunted third floor suite at the Wilbraham Mansion.

so close to them? It was one of the most relaxing naps I have ever had. Maybe ghosts should be used for insomnia!

It is true that spirits of loved ones often visit us in our dreams. It is in the dream state that we experience a "suspension of disbelief," where everything seems real. Perhaps ghosts also visit us while we are sleeping and in this state we are not afraid of them because we see them as who they were, not what they are now.

When I returned late that night from another ghost hunt in town, I waited until the other guests went to bed to start my in-house investigation. Cape May is not just a ghost magnet, it attracts scores of tourists as well. My window of opportunity to investigate in quiet is pretty narrow! There had been people swimming in the pool (yes, there is an indoor swimming pool) and I wanted to wait for a time when the house was quiet to try to contact the ghosts.

Willy and I slowly made our way down the main staircase into the parlor. It was one of two large connecting rooms that Wilbraham used to entertain his friends. In one room an enormous chandelier hung from the ceiling, reminding me of the giant swinging crystal chandelier in the 1974 movie, *The Changeling*, one of my favorite haunted house movies of all time. I moved around both parlors and the dining room before settling down in one of the Victorian chairs in the main parlor. I inhaled and exhaled, going into a meditative state. I brought the mansion's energy within me and exhaled my own energy, sending an open invitation to the ghosts of the house to join me.

I asked the ghosts to give me a sign, but there was none given. Then I focused my psychic energies a little more strongly on the house and asked verbally and psychically for the ghosts to give a "knock" if they could hear me. With that, there was a faint knock somewhere in the walls. I asked for one more, to confirm and another stronger knock followed. I could sense an older woman, and I asked her to give me a sign as to where she was. Suddenly, one of the crystal glasses in the dining room that had been set out for breakfast made a loud pinging sound—as if someone had snapped his or her finger against the bowl of the glass. There was no one else in the room, and Willy and I could find no physical cause for the glass to ping. At the same time, a cool breeze swept through the house, causing the crystals on the great chandelier to rattle. Had someone just come into the room—or had someone just left? Nothing else happened after that, and the house was quiet. We were also pretty exhausted and needed to get to bed.

When we got back up to the bedroom, I was too tired from doing an investigation elsewhere in town to set up my recording equipment. I went to bed, telling the ghosts "tomorrow" I would record them. During the night, Willy kept hearing knocking sounds in the room at various intervals. I woke up once or twice, but do not recall anything in particular waking me up. The room was very peaceful. Willy, who

164 The Wilbraham Mansion

was also sleeping in the same room, told me that I was "talking to Anne" several times during the night — talking in my sleep.

When we awoke the next morning we both noticed the small antique rocker that had been across the room by the desk had changed position. It was now much closer to the bed! A water glass from the silver tray on the dresser was also on the floor. Like living children, the two kids must have been waiting patiently for me to wake up and record them.

At breakfast, I was finally able to meet the staff. Sissy, the innkeeper, told me that the only thing she had experienced was someone in the house calling out her name. It was a woman's voice and she thought it was Patty the owner, but Patty was not home at the time and the house was empty. At the time of my first stay, Doug's mom Patty was still running the B&B. Doug and his family have since taken over the business. Ghosts often call out names of people who live in the house that they haunt.

I am not sure what the ghosts are trying to do—perhaps get the attention of someone in the living realm? They also have a knack for mimicking other living people—which can be quite unnerving when you realize the person who just called out your name is not at home.

After breakfast, I was able to speak with Patty Carnes about the house she and her family had bought in the early 1990s. I mentioned sensing an older woman who seemed to be afraid of falling down the stairs. I also got a name like "Getty" while I sat in the downstairs parlor the previous night when the knocking occurred and the glass pinged. Patty told me that the Wilbrahams had no children and after Mrs. Wilbraham died, Mr. Wilbraham's niece came to live with him in the house. "Her name may have been Betty," Patty recalled.

Psychic vision is not 20/20, nor is psychic hearing. Getty could have been *Betty* except my brain scrambled the signal just a bit. Patty told me that the niece eventually inherited the house and hired an Austrian woman as a servant. In time, the niece also passed away, childless, and left the estate to her trusted aid. Patty thought either the servant or the niece may have lived in what is now the dining room after taking a fall on the stairs and no longer wanted to take a chance climbing up the steep staircase. It seems the dining room became her bedroom, which got me to think—maybe that's why she pinged the glass in the dining room—to make sure I included her in the history part of my story.

Later, I was able to fill in some of the historical blanks. John's brother Samuel's daughter Mary Jane Wilbraham (1863-1952) moved in with her uncle at the Wilbraham Mansion after Ann's death. Ann did have grandchildren of her own who lived at the house while she was alive. After she died, it seems John's niece took over as caretaker. As the younger Miss Wilbraham got on in years, she eventually hired a companion to help her with the house. Her name was Margaret Moore, and she was a servant with Samuel Wilbraham's family in Philadelphia. After Samuel's wife, Jane, died in 1920, it seems that her daughter Mary Jane and her servant Margaret moved to Cape May to take care of John Wilbraham.

John William Wilbraham died on August 19, 1922 and the house was left to Mary Jane. When Mary Jane died on October 8, 1952, she left the mansion to her beloved caretaker, Margaret Moore (1889-1978.) Moore had even changed her last name to Wilbraham at that point! It is reported that the rest of the family was quite upset when the servant got the estate in Cape May. Moore died in February of 1978, ending the Wilbraham's reign of the mansion. I have often felt that Margaret might be hanging around the old place as well, but on the first floor.

Unfortunately, the Wilbrahams seem to have taken their history with them when they passed on. Very little was known about the family when I first started investigating the house for ghosts.

John William Wilbraham owned a foundry in Philadelphia and lived in the Frankford section of the city. In his day, he was quite a successful industrialist. I needed to find out something about the Wilbrahams, so I started making inquiries around West Cape May.

I already knew that in the mid-to-late-1800s, Cape May had a special railway that ran from what is now Wilbraham Park all the way the point to at what is today Sunset Beach. It brought passengers from the ferry landing which used to be near where the sunken ship is today. One day I was talking to Lenanne about the old railway and Wilbraham and she mentioned I should give their neighbor Marie Iaconangelo a call for she knew more about the house.

I contacted Marie by phone and, as it turned out, she is quite the font of information when it came to West Cape May. Marie told me the decorative iron fence that lines the front edge of the property was made at John Wilbraham's foundry. She also said that Wilbraham had a private spur added to the railway that went to a loading platform on the west side of the house and even had his own private rail car to pick up guests coming into the landing at the point! Unfortunately, it seemed even Marie had little to offer about the Wilbrahams history. They had faded into obscurity with time.

I later spoke with former West Cape May resident and historian Ann Pratt to whom Patty had referred me for more on the Wilbra-

hams. Ann had done extensive research on the family, but that was over ten years ago and she could not locate her notes easily. She did tell me that Wilbraham left the triangular shaped piece of parkland in front of the house to West Cape May in his will. His property was vast and he used to graze his horses on the fields near his house. Ann had also worked in the mansion years ago when the Downs owned it, and when Patty bought the property. She told me she never had any paranormal experiences while she was in the house. Oh well — you can't win them all.

Patty Carnes, on the other hand, told me that she had occasionally experienced "a feeling" in certain places in the house. This "feeling" is the way many people sense ghosts. It is not visual or audible, but feels like someone else is in the room with you. This may have been what Patty was sensing.

With any ghost investigation comes a series of mysteries. The Wilbraham Mansion was also laden with historical mysteries. I turned to my friend Jim Campbell, one of Cape May's best historians, for help.

If the Wilbrahams did not have any children — who were the two child ghosts and who was the Ann who appeared with them?

Lenanne had shown me a property deed that Dr. Albert Stevens received when he bought his plot of land in the early 1900s. The property at the time belonged to the Sheppard family.

The original farmhouse, that is now part of the mansion, was built around 1840. Wilbraham apparently lived in it in the late 1800s and then, when he permanently retired from Philadelphia to Cape May, built his grand mansion in the early 1900s. He built this grand new home in front of and around the old farmhouse.

While I was researching the rest of the West Cape May haunts, I found a common thread in all of these properties. As I mentioned in the introduction, until it was incorporated in 1884, what is now West Cape May was known as Eldredge.

Abner Corson (1729-1799) and his wife, Jane Cresse (1735-1772) purchased a 59-acre tract of land from James Whilldin, the grandson of Joseph Whilldin. Abner Corson in turn sold the tract to his daughter, Judith (1759-1831) and her husband, William Eldredge (1759-1808.)

In Judith Eldredge's will from 1833, she divides up the land along the east side of Broadway, at the time called Cape Island Road, between her children and grandchildren.

Her daughter, Judith Hughes (1790-1866) wife of Richard Hughes (1786-1850) inherited a large piece of property northwest of West Perry Street, where the Wilbraham Mansion and Albert Stevens Inn now sit. I think it was Richard and Judith Hughes who built the old farmhouse on the property in the 1830s or 40s, after they inherited the land.

The property with the farmhouse next went to Judith and Richard Hughes' daughter Judith Eldredge Hughes (1818-1860) and her husband Israel Leaming (1808-1878.)

Jim Campbell added that Judith and Israel Leaming's daughter, Abigail Hughes Leaming (1840-1889) and her husband, Dr. William Rose Sheppard (1831-1879) inherited the house and property next and lived there in the mid to late 1800s. Got that? There will be a quiz at the end of this chapter.

Patty had heard that the Hughes family owned the property originally, so this now proves correct.

Jim Campbell also told me the Sheppards had many children. One of those children, William Jr., was a real estate agent in town, and with his wife Elida, sold the property after dividing it up, once his parents had died. Albert Stevens bought his piece and John Wilbraham bought his section from the younger Sheppard and hence created a common bond between the two historic properties.

Now — you wonder why it is so difficult to figure out who is haunting a 150+ year old house? Just look at the change of ownership! In one section of the house we have family history dating back to the 1830s, with multiple generations living under the same roof. At least in Wilbraham's newer addition, it was basically he and his family living there over the years.

So, I now knew a lot about the Eldredge-Hughes connection, plus they were old Cape May stock, but what about those Wilbrahams?

There is only one place to look for physical clues of the dead—the cemetery!

My search took me to Philadelphia, to the Frankford section that Wilbraham came from. There documents abound, as Wilbraham was a huge philanthropist. Records indicate that the Frankford Hospital, in an effort to expand in 1904, paid Wilbraham's estate $38,000 for the property. Wilbraham was still alive at the time, and he had also donated money to the hospital. One of the huge crystal chandeliers in the mansion in Cape May is said to have been a gift to John Wilbraham from the hospital for his generosity towards them.

My niece, Kiersten, was getting married in July of 2006, and we stayed outside of Philadelphia. I thought this was the perfect opportunity to visit the Wilbrahams (or what was left of them) at their final resting place—the North Cedar Hill Cemetery on Frankford Avenue. It was a warm and sunny summer weekend as we made our way up Frankford Avenue.

First, I tried to find Wilbraham's old mansion, which I had heard was now part of the hospital. Calls and emails to the hospital's communications department asking for information on Wilbraham went unanswered. I wonder why they bother to call it a "communications department?"

Willy and I drove around for over an hour, but we could not find the mansion. I learned only recently that Frankford Hospital had demolished it during an expansion a few years ago.

Next it was on to the old cemetery. Knocking at the door of the caretaker's office, I was not sure what I would find, however, the gentleman who oversees the cemetery could not have been more gracious and helpful. Not only did he lead us to all of the Wilbraham plots, he pulled out all of the burial records for me! Sometimes ghost investigating can be a thankless job. Many people at first balk when I try to obtain historical information to work into a ghost story. Luckily, there are also many open-minded souls like the caretaker at North Cedar Hill.

When he took us to the large Wilbraham plot, I was finally able to solve another mystery. There on the giant obelisk, engraved in the

Opposite: The Wilbraham plot in Philadelphia (Photo by Willy Kare)

grey granite, was *John W. Wilbraham (1833-1922)* and underneath *Ann Wilbraham (1840-1916.)* Mrs. Wilbraham's name was *Ann.* I had found my ghost!

Reviewing the records, I also found out why a childless Ann Wilbraham would be haunting around the house with two children — she was remarried. Her first marriage was to Thomas Wilbraham (1827-1892.) Thomas was John's older brother and when he died in 1892, Ann married her brother-in-law John. Ann and Thomas had six children, including three who died young. I had my ghosts, but I could not find their names as the cemetery deed just mentioned that "Wilbraham children" were moved from another plot and buried in the main vault.

I had intended to include the Wilbraham Mansion in *Book 1*, but at the time I had not yet found their graves. Now, having the complete picture, I returned to the Wilbraham Mansion in February 2007 for another visit. This time Doug Carnes, Patty's son, was in charge of the house, and he graciously allowed me to walk through the mansion, tape recorder in hand.

Up the winding staircases we went — taking a slow pace so as not to disturb the ghostly inhabitants. I stopped at various points to marvel at just how beautiful the inside of the mansion was — a true Victorian treasure. We began our visit in the third floor suite, also called Room 10. Gerry Eisenhaur was along with us with his technical equipment.

As we started the equipment the tape recorder batteries suddenly drained. They *were* new batteries when I got there! With the recorder reloaded with fresh batteries I began to question Ann Wilbraham, now that I suspected it was she haunting the house.

I addressed Ann Wilbraham directly and told her I now knew who she was. As I spoke there was a very clear woman's voice saying, "John." After that there was silence, nothing, no responses to my questions. Why do ghosts do this? A perfectly clear EVP and then — *poof!* They're gone. There was a very faint EVP of a woman's voice and then a man's voice followed, but I could not make out what they said.

Psychically, as I stood in Room 10, I felt the ghosts had left. Something put the thought in my head that they "were eating." It is a com-

mon misconception to think that ghosts hang around the same spot 24/7 and go "Boo." They are social creatures. We are all souls and souls will interact with other souls, disembodied or not. Exactly what these ghosts are "eating" is a mystery to me. I am sure when we die and cross over, the paranormal picture becomes a lot clearer. I just hope in my tenure as a ghost writer, I don't piss off too many folks in the ghost realm by the time it's my turn to cross. I can picture hoards of angry Cape May ghosts shaking my books in my face shouting, "How could you write this about me!" Let's hope I put enough good light on the ghosts that they will take all of my psychic probing and prodding—in good spirits.

As for the ghosts of the Wilbraham Mansion, they certainly have a great place to spend their afterlife. I would recommend a stay here for the living as well if you want to experience a taste of the Victorian good life—with a few leftover Victorians to help make you feel right at home! This is one of Cape May's historical gems that all should enjoy.

Highland House
ROOM WITH A BOO
131 North Broadway - West Cape May

WEST CAPE MAY is a treasure trove of historical buildings. Spared from the great fires that ravaged Cape May in the late 1800s, some of West Cape May's buildings date back to Colonial times. One of those buildings, Highland House, could easily be overlooked, hidden behind a facade of added porches and well manicured gardens. I admit I missed it each time I drove along Broadway heading out of Cape May, and it was not until I heard rumors of ghostly activity at Highland House that I actually took time out to find the place.

Jim Labrusciano had first tipped me off to Highland House in the fall of 2006, when I was planning on creating a new West Cape May ghost tour with MAC. I had long wanted to include West Cape May in my stories as the entire area is too often overlooked by the tourist community and the press.

I arrived at Highland House with Willy and Gerry on President's weekend of 2007. Owner Dave Ripoli greeted us at the door, as did his pack of bouncy puppies! It is a pet friendly inn. I must admit, reviewing the tapes to write the chapter about this investigation was truly a challenge. Every time I got enough silence on the tape to grab a few EVPs — WOOF! I love dogs, I really do, but between his dogs barking and my dogs at home barking when they heard his dogs barking — I thought I would lose my mind. I love the idea of a pet friendly inn, as I think it solves a dilemma that affects all of us pet owners — what happens if we can't find a pet sitter we can trust? Places like Highland House and Billmae Cottage in Cape May offer the best of both worlds, a wonderful place to stay in Cape May *and* the pups can come with you! But, I dogress.

Highland House has had a reputation for having a ghost for a long time. When Dave bought the house, he only found out about the "extra guest" at the closing. When you buy a 150 year-old house, you have to expect there might be something kicking around in the attic—and there was.

Originally thought to have been built in 1855, there is now evidence that the original section is 1820s. This house is part of Cape May's earliest history—and some of that early history is still around to tell its story!

One cold winter evening, Dave was working all alone in the house. He had been painting the rooms and the house was empty so he decided to sleep in one of the back bedrooms. As he lay in bed trying to fall asleep, the large wicker chair next to the bed began to creak.

"It sounded just like someone was sitting in the chair. I had painted the windows shut and hadn't broken the seal yet, so there were no windows open to cause a draft," Dave recalled.

As he listened, the sound grew stronger. The noise continued for the next 10 or 15 minutes. Someone or something was sitting next to his bed in the old wicker chair. Dave promptly bolted from he room and slept on the couch that night.

It seems many have experienced the ghosts at Highland House as Dave told us the story about his very first tenants.

"In the first couple of years that I owned the house, I had a woman and her son living in the house in the lower rooms. She was here about three weeks when I stopped by to see how they were doing. I asked them how everything was and she said, 'Everything's fine except you didn't tell me you have a ghost.' And I said, 'Who did?' I didn't want to tell her anything like that. And she said 'no one told us but we heard furniture moving around up above us.' She looked outside for my car thinking I was upstairs, but I wasn't. I went up and checked the room and nothing was out of place."

The sound of furniture moving around is more common in a haunting than one may think. I have never suspected the furniture is actually physically changing location. Instead, what is being heard below is some form of energy impact on our plane coming from the ghost realm. Like the sound waves that a summer thunderstorm generates, ghosts can sometimes create their own "thunderstorm" of sound. A door opens and the energy comes through from the ghost realm — with its own sound track! At least that's *my* theory and, of course, there have been times when I have actually found the furniture *has* been moved — it is just not very often that it happens.

"The woman that owned the house before me — she told me she called him (the ghost) the fisherman's Captain. She used to refer to the ghost with her husband."

Dave also had a crew in from Philadelphia working on the house for a few days that had some experiences of their own. After hearing constant footsteps and noises in other parts of the house, the crew, who had worked on many of Philadelphia's row houses, assumed it was a family living next door. They soon realized there was no "next door," but there was indeed a *next plane!*

We made our way down the old hallway to the heart of Highland House's haunting. Every haunted house has an epicenter of energy and for Highland House the "Room with a Boo" is definitely it.

After Dave bought the place he was outside working on a ladder when a family rolled up in their car and announced that their grandmother, who was with them, used to own the home years ago. Dave invited the family in to see the work he had done. As they visited the second floor bedrooms, there was one particular room that the Grandmother refused to enter.

"I've been told that there was someone passed away in here, but I don't know how true that was," Dave told us referring to the back bedroom, "She was two owners prior to me, this woman and her family that showed up, and when I walked her through the house she stood there and said, 'the room's beautiful, but I won't go into that room — it's spooked.' The granddaughter said, 'you mean haunted?' The grandmother said, 'you call it what you call it. I'm not going in that room!'"

As I mentioned earlier, dogs and cats can see or sense ghosts, and at Highland House, this particular room proves that theory.

"I have had people who have been in here with their dogs who have actually had to pull the dogs in once they get to the doorway."

There was a point in the tape where we were entering the bedroom and no one was talking. I was able to extract three different voices from the segment. The first, child's voice says, "My room!"

This is followed by an adult male saying, "Dave knows all of the rooms."

The last voice sounds like a woman responding, but I could not make out what she was saying. The three voices came in at three different speeds. This is typical for EVP recordings. I have recorded two ghosts talking and they are each coming in at different speeds. It will be nice when science finally figures out why this is happening!

I asked Dave how long it took him to find out his new house had some "extras." He had owned the house for almost 13 years at the point of our interview in February of 2007. Some haunted homeowners never figure out they have a ghost. It is baffling, but we humans are in denial about a lot of things. Ghosts can be one of them.

"At settlement—the woman that owned the house, she told me. And then when I went to the bank, a week or so later to set up an automatic payment plan—the bank manager—she kind of looked uncomfortable with the address. I said to her 'what's up with that?' She said, 'you know the story that— that house is haunted?' I told her I just found that out at settlement. I said, 'what do you know about it?' and she just smiled. She didn't give me any details.

Dave told me that in the beginning, "it was a kind of freaky thing, but then there was nothing." The ghosts had completely quieted down. This happens many time with a change of ownership. It takes the ghosts some time to get used to new people in their home and vice versa. Eventually, both parties usually choose to coexist peacefully. Although, there have been several occasions in Cape May where the new owners do not stay long once they find out they are not alone in their new home.

Being a pet lover, I told Dave this is kind of like a dog running up to a stranger and sniffing them and getting all hyper and eventually calming down. Ghosts do chill out for the most part and go about their business. I have found the living are the ones who tend to stay uptight about a haunting.

We moved into the "Burgundy Room" and I immediately felt a presence. Even Willy, who usually does not sense these things, told Dave, "I feel like someone is in here."

I felt the presence of an older woman with white hair and almost cloudy eyes, as if she had cataracts. I kept getting the name "Dot," which could be short for Dorothy.

At the same time two voices appear on tape. A woman says, "Please tell them."

Followed by a man saying, "John Wool" or "John Wolk."

Dave continued to tell us about one woman in the room who saw something, either a figure or some form of energy in the corner of that room. He could not recall specifically what the woman saw, but remembered she had been referred by another guest, and she contacted him later to relate the experience. As Dave and I were talking a whole series of EVPs popped up on the tape.

Several EVPs sounded like women or children, but slowing them down I realized they were just a man's voice coming in fast and high pitched. A man says, "Pray for him."

This is followed by a woman replying, "We are helping him."

After that there is a shrill sound and finally another woman says, "You are a psychic." I assumed she was referring to me, ironic that even as a psychic I was having trouble hearing here, but that's the way it works sometimes—especially if there are multiple living people around me crowding the airwaves with their own energy.

Another woman says, "You will get through." I am not sure, but I think she was talking to one of the other ghosts who was trying to communicate with me. The presence in the room that I was feeling was a woman. Does a ghost have to try to make communication first for a psychic medium to sense them clearly?

Two more names, "Pool" and "Nancy" were given to me as I walked around the second floor. I walked through several other rooms, but did not pick up any extra energy. The energy in the house seems to be concentrated in one or two rooms on the second floor.

Listening to the tape, it really sounded like a group of ghosts or spirits were trying to get a channel open to communicate with me. Unfortunately, Dave's Mom had a radio on downstairs which polluted the tape's background noise for part of the tour and his four barking dogs were not helping either. Always remember to turn off all radios, televisions and dogs *before* you start taping for EVPs!

Searching through Dave's historical papers on the house and a list of owners of the property dug up by Mike Conley of House Tales, I could not find one mention of a Dorothy or a Dot.

According to Mike Conley's research on the property that he did for Dave a few years back, Judith Eldredge's estate was at one time part of James Whilldin's vast Cape May plantation. Judith's father, Abner Corson, had purchased several tracts from Whilldin and eventually left the land to his children.

Judith Eldredge gave a one-acre piece of land to her son William Eldredge on February 18, 1822, while she was still alive. It seems that several of the children were living on the big property in West Cape May (Eldredge) because in her will she mentions her son Thomas' house "where he lives today." This house is now The Eldredge House B&B featured in the next chapter.

Judith's son, William Eldredge, died a year after his mother, in 1832. In Judith Eldredge's will, dated September 21, 1833, her lands were divided up in sevenths, going to her six surviving children and the minor children of William, now deceased. His children were Albert, Elizabeth C., George and Malvina.

October 23, 1850, Albert, Elizabeth and George Eldredge, the children of William Eldredge, sold their shares of the property to their brother-in-law Jacob Leaming and sister Malvina Leaming. The land and premises were known as "William Eldredge Place."

On August 4, 1852 Jacob and Malvina Leaming sold to Sabina E. Bauersack "all that house and tract of land." If you recall the chapter about the Jacob Leaming House, this is the same Malvina and Jacob Leaming. Everyone in Cape May was related back in those days! From there the property changed hands many times.

There are several stumbling blocks when one investigates a haunting in a historical house like Highland House. Old buildings like this one usually had dozens of owners over a 150 year period. Compound that with most houses in Cape May doubling as private residences and boarding houses, and the ghostly trail goes off in twenty different directions!

Is the ghost of the elderly woman who is haunting Highland House an Eldredge? Who were the other ghostly voices caught on tape? Standing in that back bedroom was like hooking into a phone line to the Other Side!

In March of 2008, a year after my first visit to Highland House, I decided the investigation needed a follow up. Willy, Gerry and I met Dave Ripoli at the house, and I immediately cut to the chase and headed for the "Blue Room" on the second floor, also called the "spooked room" by the previous owner.

After banishing Dave and Willy to the lower floor (they would not stop yapping) Gerry and I set up the video camera and the cassette tape recorder in the room.

I was not feeling anything in particular, just the room's mix of energies. I asked the ghosts to come forward and speak on the tape — and they did.

I barely had the tape recorder turned on when background voices appeared in the white noise. I found the first EVP segment contained three different voices — like the first recording a year earlier. A man's voice is heard first, but the words do not make any sense. Either he says, "You're teasin' him on the radio," or something to that effect.

A woman's voice then says, "He will catch me!"

I think the ghosts may be thinking that I was carrying a small radio instead of a tape recorder. Maybe they understood one, but not the other. My feeling was that they felt I was listening to them over a radio and one was making sounds via EVPs to tease me and another felt that I would somehow "catch" her.

When I asked the ghosts to give me their names, a man mentioned "the silver" and then says, "her other father."

The segment ends with a woman pleading, "Help me please!"

I felt they were playing with me on tape. Some of the words made sense, but they were strung together to form bizarre sentences. The deeper voiced man even tried to create a frightening persona for himself on tape, which might have worked if they had not already mentioned they were going to "tease me."

The psychic feeling here is that one of the ghosts, one of the men, does not want to be bothered by the living, and he can create a feeling of forboding inside whomever he encounters. Maybe this is a defense mechanism that ghosts have, like a skunk's spray. Ghosts repel the living with negative feelings that the living then absorb and take as their own. It did not work on me and I was going to continue my investigation. I think this is the reason one of the previous owners felt the room was "spooked." In fact, nothing happened to us while we visited each time. It was just a nice, blue guest room—with lots of ghostly voices—should one be running a tape recorder. Anyone interested in the paranormal should get on the phone, call Dave and book this room for a few nights—this room paranormally rocks!

Communication is a one way affair when an investigator relies strictly on the results of EVPs. I first use my psychic ability to tune, then I run some tapes as backup. If I am lucky, the energies will be strong enough for my psychic information to match my EVP evidence.

Opposite: The famous "spooked" Blue Room (photo by Gerry Eisenhaur)

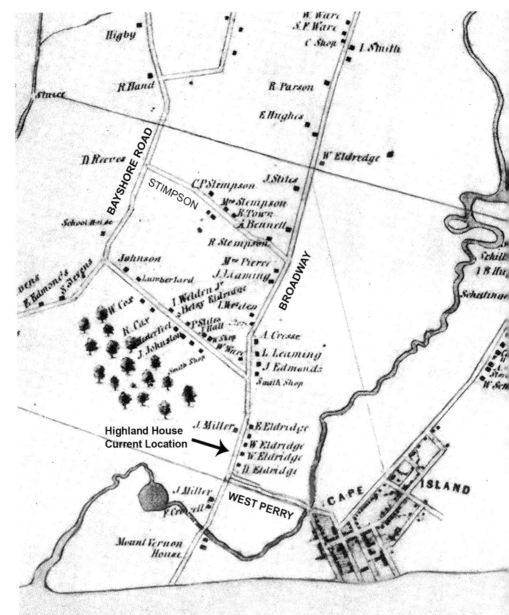

PART OF NUMAN'S 1850 MAP OF CAPE MAY

By reviewing the earlier investigation's tapes, I knew approximately how many entities and what types of ghosts I was dealing with in the Blue Room. Because I could not hear them during the second session, as I was not able to completely tune in psychically, (I was exhausted from a busy weekend at The John F. Craig House) I addressed them in a sort of one-way communication. I knew with whom I was dealing, I just did not know their responses. However, knowing the types of personalities allowed me to texture the questions in a certain way that might prevent them from walking out in the middle of the interview!

It was time to start the history lesson with the ghosts. "Are you descendents of William Eldredge?" I asked them.

"No," was a man's response, followed by what I thought was, "enough." After I listened to the tape numerous times and removed more and more hiss and boosted the volume of what was left, the word became crystal clear. It was not "enough" it was "Enoch." Enoch Eldredge was William's brother!

Enoch Eldredge (1779-1839) was the oldest sibling of William (1759-1808) and Judith (1759-1831) Eldredge. His piece of Judith's estate was north of Thomas' slice of land. It was up the road from where the Highland House now sits. As I mentioned earlier, I thought Highland House was built in 1855, but Mike Conley recently told me they now think sometime in the 1820s is a more accurate date. This fact came to light after the new Historic Survey was completed. This would make more sense since the Eldredge kin are haunting this house.

William Eldredge Place, as that piece of Judith's estate was called, may have had an earlier dwelling on the site. On the 1850 Numan Map of Cape May (see opposite page) there are several Eldredge dwellings near the spot where Highland House sits today. I think one of the "W. Eldredge" houses on the map is Highland House.

If we look at the bigger paranormal picture here, what we have is a large estate that housed generations of Eldredges over a 200+ year period. My guess is that when family members started dying off, something pulled some of them back to the old homestead. As with any large, extended family living next door to one another, fences and borders are usually overlooked for a greater sense of communal living. This was Eldredge land and no one was going to take it away from them. At least as far as the dead Eldredges go. Some just have not left.

On the tape, when I started naming members of the Eldredge clan who I felt were associated with the house, I mentioned William C. Eldredge a response on the tape said, "William's here."

William C. Eldredge (1820-1905) was actually Enoch's son, so it would make sense if the ghosts were tied to Enoch, he might be haunting the place as well. At this point my head was spinning with Eldredges. So many dead Eldredges — how would I tell which ones were haunting this particular house?

I asked the ghosts if it was the "spooked room" that I was in and there was absolutely no response. I guess they didn't like that one. Next I asked if the ghosts were not Eldredges, if they were later owners of the house.

The response was a sad, "Nobody wants to live forever." It was not an appropriate answer to my question, but it was an interesting statement to ponder — coming from a ghost.

In several instances they mention a "William." One EVP says, "William is here."

In another EVP a woman says, "They are keeping me here — William." William being a common name, it is hard to conjecture which William is haunting the house. Is it patriarch William Eldredge (1759-1808,) his son William Eldredge, Jr. (1791-1832) or is it Enoch's son William C. Eldredge (1820-1905) doing the haunting? If we go solely on the EVP evidence where the ghost says they are descended from Enoch, then it could be Enoch's son William C. Eldredge in the house. It is a bit of a mystery.

"How many ghosts are there in this house?" I asked, trying to narrow the playing field.

"They're all over," a deeper man's voice responded on tape, followed by possibly another man saying "three." There was definitely a pitch difference in the two male voices on the tapes. One voice was a deep baritone, while the other was more sharp and nasal sounding. One of them was William, the other two either did not or would not identify themselves. "They are all over" made me think we were dealing with a neighborhood of Eldredge ghosts, which is possible considering the neighborhood was once called *Eldredge!*

Another one of the male voices then said, "Go in the bathroom."

I had been through the rooms, but not the bathrooms. I unfortunately heard this instruction too late to act on the tip.

At this point I felt someone else enter the room. The door was closed, and I commented to Gerry who was standing near the doorway with the camera that I felt the entity had become almost flat or two-dimensional and folded itself through the crack in the door that was open, returning to normal shape when it was in the room. I supposed a ghost, being a field of energy, can assume any shape it wants. Maybe they exist in a more two dimensional form and that is why we cannot see them very often.

With that feeling I picked up the name "Robert" coming into the room. Gerry felt the temperature drop around him, near the door, and commented that he too felt something enter the room. Gerry is quite intuitive in his own way.

The name "Judge" popped into my head. There was a Judge Eldredge, but there was no follow up of communication, either psychic or EVP.

I decided a change in venue was in order, and I told the ghosts we would be going back to the Garden Room, the bedroom on the other side of the wall from the Blue Room. I announced, "Let's go back to the Garden Room," and then I added, "Garden Room, folks," addressing the ghosts. On the tape appears the strongest EVP of the investigation.

Between my two passages, a loudly whispered EVP says, "Get them to follow us." Either they were trying to get us going in another direction or they saw us packing up and wanted us to stay a little longer.

I sensed more activity in the beautiful Garden Room next door on the second floor. This is the room where Dave told me he had spent one of his first nights in the house, when he heard something sitting and moving around in the large wicker chair/couch near the bed. He was alone in the house that night — or so he thought!

I decided to sit in the "haunted" wicker couch and see what I could sense from that vantage point in the house. I detected children, which I had never sensed in the house prior to this visit. However, they did not interact with me, and they may have only been residual energy in the house. I also sensed someone saying the name "Charlotte."

I asked a few more questions, hoping to up my chances of getting some solid EVPs. As you can see, I have gone a little heavier in EVP recording in this book than in *Books 1 & 2*. My idea was to introduce another element of ghost investigation that may add to the paranormal evidence and create a clearer picture of each haunting. I also get bored of just doing the same old psychic thing over and over. I need to keep trying different things in my life and changing my regular routines — ghost investigating included.

I received the term "psychic orphanage" when the childrens' images popped into my head. I thought about all of the ghostly children I had encountered in Cape May and could hear Jim Campbell's words that in the mid-1800s 60% of the mortalities in Cape May were children under the age of 10. I assumed the term meant that the souls of children who choose not to cross over to Heaven eventually find their way to a sort of psychic orphanage, somewhere for adult ghosts to watch over theses lost young souls.

I asked the ghosts, "Is this a place where souls gather that are lost? Psychic orphanage was an odd term, and I was not sure if I had it completely correct.

The response was, "Yes, we are," in a man's voice.

A chorus of higher voices then added, "We're ghosts from houses." This was even more confusing. They obviously did not understand

Opposite — The Garden Room (photo by Gerry Eisenhaur)

my reference to "psychic orphanage" and just heard either, "is this where lost souls gather," or thought I said, "Are you lost souls."

From the feelings I received psychically and the EVP responses, it truly appeared that some of these ghosts did *not* want to be "stuck." I have heard ghosts cry out for help before on EVP recordings in other houses, and the lady ghost here seemed to want out.

"How close are you to Heaven?" I asked, realizing I had a strong connection with the Other Side here and that maybe they could shed some like on their whereabouts.

"Never been there," was the response of the nasal-sounding man.

I also asked, "Am I talking to people in Heaven," there was no response. The Ghost Realm seems quite isolated from Heaven.

The woman added, "Are we forgiven?" leaving me to believe they had done something they felt was keeping them Earthbound.

In Cape May I have encountered many different ghost personalities. Some tell me they stay because they like it, others will not move on because of personal reasons. I think ghosts can cross over if they want to go, but sometimes it seems other ghosts do not want them to leave. In life we become attached to people, maybe in death — should we stay earthbound—we become attached to other ghosts, and form bonds of friendship or even—romance.

I sensed another child, a boy. The name Robert came into my head again and I asked Gerry, "I wonder if the boy's name is Robert?"

A child answers back on the tape, "Yes sir."

I asked for a sign and got nothing. I think I need to get the hint at this point and stop asking for signs. Ghosts do *not* go for this at all.

On the tape an EVP says, "Let's run out into the hall." I guess they were getting tired of my prodding. After that the tape went quiet.

Highland House stands on a tract of land that has a long and rich history in West Cape May. It is a wonderful, friendly place to stay. There is a common misconception about a house that is haunted—people either think of old Hollywood movies or cheap amusement park rides when they imagine what it must be like to live in a haunted house. While some haunted places can be a bumpy ride, Highland House is not one of those places. It is a wonderful, pet-friendly inn that sits on a quiet stretch of Broadway in West Cape May within walking distance of the shops and surf.

The activity here is all caught on tape. Maybe a few bumps in the night every now and then, but the bulk of paranormal evidence is in the form of psychic communication both live and recorded. If you love the idea of ghosts or just love the quiet, relaxing beauty of Cape May—Highland House is a must stay. Dave and his Mom Terry will show you a great time.

As for all of those dead Eldredges—they are always on the move in West Cape May, and you can never tell when one will be floating in your front door! Read on.

Eldredge House

SO MANY DEAD ELDREDGES — SO LITTLE TIME

Historic Inn

417 North Broadway, West Cape May

ONE of the most fascinating things about West Cape May is that the history is so intertwined between many of the homes. Today, the name Eldredge may not mean much to anyone living or visiting town, but in its day, the Eldredge family were the movers and shakers in this neck of the woods. Some of the original players are still moving and shaking things — you just can't see them anymore. You see, they're dead, and have been for a long time.

In Cape May, death never stops anyone from having fun. For the ghosts of Cape May, death is just putting on the suntan lotion — it's just the beginning of their long sojourn by the sea. It will be some time before they pack up for good and move on to Heaven.

When I decided to expand my ghost writing to include more of West Cape May, Jimmy Labrusciano of The Albert Stevens Inn, had offered to coordinate an effort to find other homeowners or business owners in West Cape May who might be interested in being part of the new Ghost Trolley Tour. He came up with a list of about five or six people.

The first person I called was Todd Land, owner of the Eldredge House at 417 Broadway. The house was said to be one of the oldest structures in Cape May, so I thought it would be a good place to start when I needed to expand my list of haunts in West Cape May.

We made reservations at The Bedford for President's Day weekend and I had Gerry Eisenhaur stay at The Linda Lee, with his equipment to work on that investigation. Time is limited when I get down to

Cape May, so we sometimes have to cram our investigations! I decided I would spend the entire three days researching potential haunts in West Cape May. I was also on a timetable to get a script done for the new MAC West Cape May/Lighthouse Ghost Tour, so I needed to cover a lot of ground (and ghosts) fast.

I left a message for Todd on Valentine's Day of 2007, but never heard back from him. We were in the middle of a nor'easter and I thought perhaps he had lost power and could not call me back.

I had also called Diane Flanagan at Flanagan's Art Studio, across the street from Todd, and she had called me back and we set up an appointment. When I stopped by Flanagan's Art Studio, Diane told me the reason Todd had probably not returned my phone call. On Valentine's Day night Cape May got a record amount of rain in addition to gale force winds. At 2 AM, the ancient, 100-foot silver maple in front of Todd's house had blown down onto the neighbor's house! If the ghosts were trying to get him to call me back, I am sure there would have been a better way of doing it than knocking down a 200-year-old tree!

Diane was nice enough to walk us across the street and introduce us to Todd. While Todd and Diane talked in his living room, Willy, Gerry and I were allowed to walk through the house and do our impromptu ghost investigation. We loaded the tape records and moved up to the second floor of the house.

I immediately felt multiple presences on the second floor as I stood in the hallway between the three bedrooms. Gerry's camera batteries immediately drained — damn ghosts!

Willy shot some digital pictures and got numerous "orbs" which I discount as light refraction most of the time. This one picture was pretty impressive however. At the same time I asked if Thomas or Mary Eldredge were present and if they could speak with us.

According to the house history that Todd inherited, Thomas Eldredge and his sister, Mary Eldredge Hughes, both lived in the house. Todd's property is about where Mary's one-seventh slice of property is located on her mother's 1833 will/map.

196 The Eldredge House

As I mentioned in previous chapters, Judith Eldredge, matriarch of the West Cape May Eldredges, divided her land into seven parts in her will. Her father, Abner Corson, had purchased more than 59 acres from James Whilldin, Grandson of Joseph Whilldin, that stretched for miles along what is now Broadway from Cape May through West Cape May. Thanks to an in-depth Historic Properties Survey of West Cape May just completed by Joan Berkey and Mike Conley, many of the historical mysteries of the buildings in town have now been solved in the fabulous 700+ page report. It is available for everyone to use and enjoy at West Cape May Borough Hall. Kudos to Joan and Mike!

Basically, many of the haunts in West Cape May are pieces of the same original plantation first owned by Joseph Whilldin. The Moonfish Grill, featured in *Book 1*, is actually the Whilldin-Miller House. I (luckily) caught wind of the new historical survey of West Cape May before I had finished this book. The research Joan and Mike did is amazing and invaluable to anyone interested in the historic properties in town, haunted or not. Joan Berkey took the old 1833 land division map and overlaid today's tax map to line up the old properties with what exists today. I had tried to do this, but was not 100% successful.

From Joan's new/old map I could see the Eldredge House was on the land that was left to Mary Eldredge Hughes by her mother, Judith. Unfortunately, Judith's map does not show dwellings, and there is no way to know when The Eldredge House first appeared on the site.

According to Berkey and Conley's historic survey, Mary Eldredge Hughes and Judith Eldredge Hughes sold their tracts of land on Broadway to their brother Enoch shortly after they inherited it. In 1861, Enoch's son Enoch, Jr. (1822-1868) sold a piece of property with an old house on it to his first cousin, Thomas Eldredge (1835-1909.) Thomas was a Delaware River pilot and lived in the house until his death in 1909.

Eldredge House, it is thought, started as a one and one half story dwelling around 1780 somewhere else. One old story is that it was moved from Jackson Street near Lafayette. The Memucan Hughes

House was also thought to have been moved from this area to its current location on Washington Street (see *Book 2*.)

At some point in the 1820s or 1830s, the house was raised to a two story structure. Eventually, the house and another house were moved to where the final Eldredge House sits today.

So, basically what I had to work with was a house that was originally two different houses and had also been added onto over the course of the nineteenth century. The oldest section being almost 230 years old! This house was a crazy quilt of energy, and I was definitely *wearing it.*

Todd told us that he had named the two bedrooms on the second floor "Thomas' Room" and "Mary's Room," for the brother and sister who had lived in the house. Now, with the historic survey information and an in-depth report on Eldredge House by Joan Berkey, it is now clear that many Eldredges lived in the house. We know all about the history of the land. The problem is no one is sure when *the house* arrived!

My guess is that William and Judith Eldredge, who were married on December 10, 1778, built the house when they got married. It was then moved to a new tract that Judith Eldredge bought from her father, Abner Corson.

Berkey and Conley's Historic Property Survey reveals that in August of 1789, the late Joseph Whilldin's grandson, James, sold a 59-acre tract located on the east side of what is now known as Broadway to Abner Corson. A few months later, Abner Corson sold the tract to his daughter, Judith, and her husband, William Eldredge for £103. The Eldredge House house stands on part of that tract. If William and Judith did live in the small house on Jackson Street, they would have surely relocated to their new 59 acre tract to the north, and taken their house with them.

In those days, as I have mentioned before in *Book 1* and *Book 2*, labor was cheaper than lumber and hardware. Therefore, I think the Eldredges moved the 1½ story dwelling up Broadway and parked it on their new plantation. They most likely expanded the house as more children arrived.

While the north wing of the Eldredge House is thought to have been built in 1780 or later, the south wing is newer, being built around 1830. It is unknown who was living in the house at this time. Judith Eldredge died in 1831 and the property was divided in 1833, but she had previously sold small lots to her children over the years. Judith spent her final years in a house that may today be 113 Myrtle Avenue, according to Berkey and Conley's report, so Judith did not live in the "Eldredge House" at the time of her death.

My thought is that since her daughter, Mary Eldredge Hughes (1785-1863,) wife of Israel Hughes (1778-1833) inherited this tract, with the house, after her mother's death, she may have already been living on the property. I am not sure what happened after she sold it to her brother Enoch. He was already living next door.

Israel's father was Memucan Hughes (1739-1812) and he is thought to have built the Colonial House/Memucan Hughes House that now stands behind Alexander's on Washington Street. That house is also thought to have been moved from Jackson Street. Could both houses have, at one time, been next door to each other on Jackson Street?

According to Berkey and Conley's report, an old 1894 newspaper article titled *The Eldredges of West Cape May, NJ* that appeared in the *Star of the Cape* on June 29, 1894, stated that William Eldredge 'built his dwelling house' on a lot he purchased from Thomas Hand on Cape Island (Cape May City.) The report theorizes, "this probably refers to the lot he bought adjacent to the bridge over Cape Island Creek in 1795 from Thomas Hughes (who had purchased it from Thomas Hand.)"

This information all seems to point to a Hughes family link to the original house. Only time or ghosts will tell and, since this is a book on ghosts with a little history thrown in, I will now move on to the original reason we are here: Who is haunting the Eldredge House?

We had gathered in the second floor hallway outside of Thomas Eldredge's bedroom in the old, north wing. This is the room that was

An old farmhouse in West Cape May — possibly the original section of today's Eldredge House. (Courtesy of Todd Land)

originally only a half-story high sleeping chamber for the house, but it was the oldest part and a great place to start the investigation.

The cassette tape recorder was started and as I asked for the ghosts to speak with us, there was a *crystal clear,* Class A, EVP of a young child crying. It sounded to us like a toddler, maybe two or three years old. The child cried. Gerry's camera is heard snapping pictures and then the child cries again. One of the best EVPs I have ever recorded — or so I thought.

After Gerry and I were both convinced of a baby crying, he compared the video tape to the audio tape where the baby cries. The phantom baby, as it turned out, was the automatic lens opening and closing on Gerry's camera. He *had* to bring a camera that sounded like a dead baby crying! So, the baby (EVPs) get thrown out with the bath water in this case. Always make sure your EVPs are not caused by something living.

A child's voice *is* heard on the tape in the beginning however and that is not associated with a camera. Todd told me that, in the old days, the front section of the house used to be a nursery which stretched between the two bedrooms. The Eldredges did have several children die at a young age.

One EVP in a child's voice overlays Willy speaking in the very beginning saying, "I'm gonna take a nap." Why can't the ghosts nap *before* I get there?

Another EVP says, "Find me." This sounds like the same child. Short nap.

We moved into the Mary's bedroom next. This is upstairs on the second floor in the oldest part of the house. Gerry's EMF meter went from zero up to 0.4, which is not a huge increase, but for a stationary reading it could mean something in the ambient energy field was changing. As he mentioned the meter jumping, I had been feeling that something came into the room with us. It was a male presence. For the record, I did not sense a child at this point in the investigation.

A man's voice appears in the background noise of the tape saying, "He'll find us," along with another voice saying, "Craig's a psychic."

I would love to know how the ghosts can totally observe us and read us like a book, while we can barely sense them at all. The human-ghost relationship is definitely a one way street!

I started to sense the name "George." The feeling of a man with that name got stronger as I stood in the old bedroom. George felt like he had lived in the house for a long time and he mentioned "gardens in back." His personality felt like it did not want us bothering him, that he would cooperate and talk with us only briefly. Then it felt like we were annoying him.

Todd later contacted Jean Davis, a previous owner of the house who still lives in the area. She thought she remembered a George with the house two owners prior to her tenure at the house. She also felt he may have been an Eldredge and enjoyed gardening.

After I mentioned the name George to the group, the EVP levels on the tape started to go nuts. As I sensed a George, a higher-pitched man's voice is heard speaking to an older man who sounds like he is in his 80s.

The younger man mentions something like, "We have to get in his car" and then says, "we can't be discovered." I hope they weren't planning a getaway.

George really had a fix on me. The EVP following my question, "Is there anyone here with us," comes through in a man's voice saying, "This guy spoke to me." He was talking to another ghost, but that voice was muffled.

The other voice also may have been a female voice, but it was hard to tell. It is not a good idea to over manipulate the EVP recordings. If you have a good ear, you can get the speed and pitch right and reveal the sound of the ghost's true voice. If the EVP is faint or muffled (Class B or C) and requires levels of manipulation to be clear, that extra editing may not only change the voice, but the meaning of the words as well. There is a great website for this — *www.aaevp.com*.

I try to pick out what is being said, *before* I manipulate the sound track in Adobe Audition®, my sound editing program. If I am lucky enough to catch a Class A EVP that can be heard clearly by anyone, without using headphones, I will leave the EVP in tact and not edit it at all.

I asked if it was his bedroom, and he told me that it was. On tape an EVP clearly says, "old days." He was also mentioning to me that he was upset about his silver tree falling down.

I was having trouble putting a time stamp on George. At that point I was not sure which George Eldredge I was speaking with. Judith's son William Jr. had a son George, but he would have been born around 1820 and was certainly not the same George as Jean had mentioned. The older George Eldredge may have lived in the house at some point, but I could find no birth or death dates for him at the time of this writing.

There were several voices on the tape, so I may have been communicating with two different entities at once. The only name I was getting at the time was George — who became a little agitated with my constant probing and made a few derogatory remarks toward us — one of which was caught on tape.

"Why did you come here?" he asked in an EVP.

This was followed by another more pleasant toned man who asks, "Do you need my company?"

Still, George was getting annoyed and we needed to go. I thought it best to move on to the bedroom on the other side of the house. At the time I did not realize this was once a completely different house!

As we started to cross the hallway between the bedrooms, I felt the presence of a young child around me. The child kept saying the name, "Hattie." We moved into "Thomas' Room," named for Captain Thomas Eldredge, the second floor bedroom on the south side front of the house.

I situated myself on a chair by the wall as Gerry set up some equipment. The name kept repeating, causing me to ask the girl if she were telling me her name. We sat and waited. We rewound the tape and checked for EVPs. The word "window" kept repeating. We looked out the window, but all we could see was the stump of the 300-year-old Silver Maple below and a quiet Broadway and sleepy winter West Cape May beyond.

After a few minutes Gerry pulled out the EMF (electro-magnetic field) meter and scanned the room. Most of the room read zero until he moved near the front window. The meter started to spike and hit between 3 and 5 on the scale, finally peaking at 18 and then returning to zero. The electrical supply to the house does come in near that corner of the building, but the reading should have been steady. Ghosts are thought to drain energy for their own use from other EMF sources and power lines are their number one delicacy.

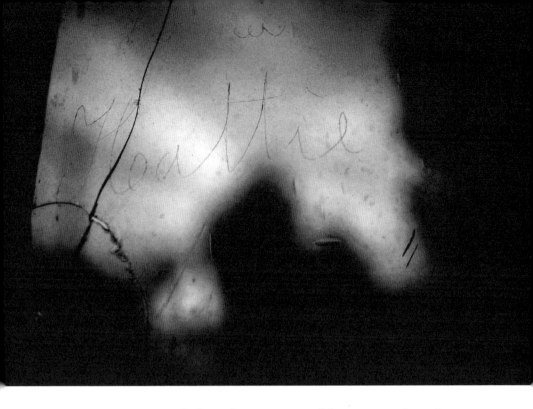

Etched in history — and glass, the names, possibly James, and Hattie appear on the bedroom window in Mary's Room at the Eldredge House.

"Tree," I heard the child say. I told Gerry to look at the tree again. As he focused in the large brown stump, something else came into his field of view. In the window in front of him, etched in the glass, were the names James and *Hattie!* The etching was so fine that the daylight had made it impossible for us to see, until it was viewed against the dark background of the tree stump below. Gerry decided to do a rubbing of the etching and later, I had Maciek (everyone calls him Magic) fly in from Poland and work his photographic "magic" on a good shot that we could reproduce for the book (see above.)

At the time Gerry was doing his pencil and paper rubbing of the glass with Willy, Todd and I were walking around another section of the house. Todd's friend Peter had arrived and was telling me about the history of the house. On the tape, a sing-song like voice of a child says something to Gerry, but it is impossible to tell what the child is saying. This EVP is loud, but not clear. The energy of a child was very strong in the house. There were no living children, so I could safely assume I was sensing a ghost. It was not a residual energy—it was changing and interacting with us and the equipment.

I asked Todd if he had any experiences with a child ghost.

"My Mom, my aunt, two guests, all those are the consistent experiences," Todd told me. It seemed his Mom had the most frequent encounters with the ghosts when she slept in Mary's Room or cleaned the house. "My Mom sees—has seen, a small woman, child or man. She says she gets confused because she thinks it's a girl and then it's a guy—this usually happens when she is cleaning the house—about the only thing that always happens is the cleaning fluids keep getting knocked over."

I felt that Todd's Mom was encountering both George and Hattie, but at different times.

"My mom said that she and my aunt were sleeping in this bed one night, and they woke up to somebody tapping at their toes—my aunt said I thought it was a woman, my Mom said she couldn't tell."

While George is psychically strong, he remains heard, yet unseen. The child, however, seems to have the ability to manifest into an apparition. She is usually seen by people as they wake up to find her making noise in the room and she quickly vanishes.

With a B&B, Inn or historic hotel, sometimes the best barometer of ghosts are the guests themselves.

"I had one guest say to me—'Is this house haunted by a little girl?' and you never know what to say, and this woman was from upstate New York and she said, 'there's a little girl, and she was just here in the room.'" Apparently the guest was a little psychic, because I think you need to have some ability to witness an apparition in an awake state.

The attic was beckoning me. Something had put the image of the old upper section of the house in my mind. This is usually either a precognitive image or ghosts sending me a private invitation to join

Sometimes a cluttered attic is the perfect place for ghosts to hide.

them. I accepted the invitation and moved with the group up the old, spiral staircase.

The house was raised sometime in the mid-1800s, it is thought. So, the attic's energy was not as old as the lower sections of the house. In contrast, the back wing of the house, built around 1880, had no paranormal feeling at all. The energy was concentrated in the forward sections of the house.

There is something eerie about climbing old wooden steps to an ancient attic. Attics can actually be more frightening to me then basements. I think this is because ghosts congregate upward and not down into dark cellars. If you had a choice, would you choose to live in an attic, with windows or a dark cellar?

As we checked out the rooms in the attic — nothing happened. No energy, no energy readings on Gerry's meters, no EVPs on the tapes, nothing. I always get to ghost parties too late!

Todd told us his Mom had a priest come in to bless the house. The priest did a walk-through and felt all of the spirits were good spirits, that there was nothing bad in the house. I agree. The priest also felt the attic was clear. Hmm, a psychic priest, sounds like a cool guy.

As we stood in the second floor hallway, George made one last comment to Todd, "Stop changing the wall colors—you're driving me crazy!"

Todd was a little shocked by that comment—he admitted his Mom had been constantly changing the paint colors in the house!

I sensed George sitting all the time, like he had trouble walking or standing. Todd recalled he had heard the George who owned the house before Jean Davis, the previous owner, and had loved to garden, but he eventually had to sell the house because he could not get around and take care of it any longer. Was our ghost *that* George or an even older version?

As I have said before, the best way to investigate a haunted house is to spend the night. As long as you remain calm and focused, you should also get a good night's sleep. Unless, of course, something should try to get into bed with you. It happens.

Back we went a few months later to the Eldredge House. This time, Gerry took Thomas' Room with the etched window on the south side of the house, and Willy and I took Mary's Room in the oldest part of the house. Because this room was the epicenter of energy in the house on our previous visit—we held the séance in there that evening.

All kinds of energy was floating around once I entered a deep trance. As with any of my trance channelings, I seem to send out a psychic searchlight that just pulls the ghosts in! Someone claiming to be a Whilldin showed up, as did George and the young child.

The most interesting thing that evening was the presence of more than one dead child. There were several, and they were particularly fond of Gerry! It was quite late when we finished channeling and we were not sure if anyone else was staying in the back bedroom of the house, so we had to try to contain ourselves and the ghosts. The children kept insisting, through me, that Gerry go to the attic. The only problem is the attic was pitch black and we were afraid Gerry would either fall through the ceiling into some other room or wake the other guests sleeping below. For some reason they wanted him in the attic.

It was at this point that I felt Gerry had some previous past life connection to the house. Gerry had been feeling the energies there since we first investigated. I always told his mother, I thought that her son was psychic, which is why I started bringing him along with us in the first place (plus the fact that he *really* wanted to go ghost hunting.) Gerry's energy seemed to click with Eldredge House. I do not know what the connection is, but it's there.

When we did an investigation with The New York Daily News in October of 2007, Gerry took reporter Robert Dominguez inside the Eldredge House one evening. Willy and I waited outside and talked to Todd. Gerry had not been inside five minutes when he emerged with a tape full of EVPs!

On a recent trip back to the old homestead, with Gerry in tow, we visited Todd and his partner Ron at the Eldredge House one more time. We sat downstairs in the living room for a while and though it was just a social visit, I told Gerry we should do one quick walk through of the second floor.

After spending a few minutes in each room, I received a psychic message from the ghostly children again. "Gerry come to the attic and we will touch your face." Makes you feel all warm and fuzzy inside, doesn't it? Right.

I was told to "get out" and "go downstairs," which I promptly did, leaving Gerry to climb the old attic stairs alone. About ten minutes later Gerry arrived back in the living room, slightly stirred. It seems something *did* brush the side of his face as he sat on the floor of the attic!

So, fine, the ghosts want Gerry and not me. Not a problem at all. I can't wait to see what happens when Gerry stays there for a week with his family this spring. It will be like *The Brady Bunch* meets *13 Ghosts!* As for Hattie, or the child who first wanted us to notice the window with the name Hattie, I do think she belongs to the Eldredge family. I also believe she has a few friends who drop in to play with her every now and then.

Hattie is a nickname for Harriet. Thomas Eldredge (1835-1909) who owned the house from 1861 until his death in 1909, had a daughter Harriet Sawyer Eldredge (1861-1904.) The time frame would prove that Harriet (called Hattie throughout her life) was born the year her father bought the house from his cousin Enoch Eldredge. In those days it was common for children to etch their names in the glass panes. Hattie Eldredge was probably the one who did this. The only problem is she lived until the age of 43 and married Daniel Ezekiel Stevens (1857-1937) and they lived elsewhere. Now, Daniel Steven's just happen to be the uncle of Dr. Albert Stevens and since he is haunting around the corner, I guess anything is possible in this family! However, I think the child is a different Eldredge who died at a young age.

On of my tapes run in the house, I kept hearing a name like "Harriet." I thought this confirmed the Hattie Eldredge link, but when listening to the tapes again, I think the name actually says "Harry." The child is addressing one of the male ghosts. Since I am pretty sure George is the older sounding man on the tape, I will assume that Harry is the younger voiced man. This theory could be correct as Thomas did have a son who lived in the house named Henry (Harry) S. Eldredge who was a Delaware Bay pilot like his father and was lost at sea on March 12, 1888 at the age of 24. A traumatic death like drowning combined with vigor and youth can, certainly set the stage for a ghostly existence.

According to old records, Thomas and his wife Emma Tabitha Baker Clifton (1841-1913) also had several daughters who seemed to have died at a young age. An Elizabeth R. Eldredge (1865-) appears on the 1870 census, but disappears by the 1880 census, possibly because she died some time in the 1870s. Another daughter, Katie Eldredge, is also unaccounted for at this time. These deaths occurred during the time that Thomas and Emma lived at the Eldredge House.

There is one more interesting coincidence here. As I mentioned earlier, the Colonial House on Washington Street, now called the Memucan Hughes House, was thought to have been built around 1800 on Jackson Street, near Lafayette and later moved to Washington Street.

This house also has the distinction of being one of the only other houses in Cape May that has names etched in the windows.

The inscription etched into upstairs bedroom window of the Memucan Hughes House reads: *"Enoch Eldredge June 19th 1806 Elizabeth Eldredge."* (pictured above)

This Enoch was Thomas' uncle and Enoch's first wife, Elizabeth Stillwell, who were married in 1805 and lived in the Colonial House at the time. Elizabeth died in 1811 at the age of 24.

I think that at one point in history, the Eldredge House(s) and the Colonial House sat on the same Eldredge property somewhere on Jackson Street. The name etching was done by the same family at different times. The Colonial House is haunted, the Eldredge House is haunted. Somebody at some time sent the houses off in two different directions, and the ghostly family got divided up.

On a side note, Mary Eldredge, Enoch's sister, also married Memucan Hughes' son Israel Hughes. So there is another connection with that house and the Eldredge family. Is your head spinning yet?

The setting sun casts a ghostly glow on Hattie's window (right)

Why is all of this history and family tree material so important in a book on ghosts you might ask? I feel to truly understand a haunting that is taking place in a historic home like this one, the investigator needs eventually to research the back history. Ghosts rarely give names, at least they do not give them up easily. I got the name George, psychically. Hattie, was the name on the window which I originally mistook for the child's name. The child never gave me a name other than Hattie. The name "Harry" appears as an EVP on the tape. Without knowing the history of the previous owners, one would never know who was doing the haunting and perhaps never know why they were haunting.

History can also supply the answers to motives. A ghostly child usually haunts a place where it lived and felt safe or an area where it last resided while it was alive. A young man, Harry in this case, dies on the Delaware Bay and his soul returns home to be with his young wife and family at his father's home. If we did not know Thomas had a son who followed in his footsteps as a ship's pilot, and drowned at sea, we might never know why a man named Harry haunted the house.

George, being more recent in history, was remembered by living witnesses. First hand accounts are always a great way to record history. I just wish it was done more often!

The Eldredge House is another hidden gem in Cape May. All of these virtually unknown, great places to stay exist in West Cape May within walking distance of the beach and the shops. While they are usually off the radar of most tourists coming to Cape May, the Inns and B&Bs of West Cape May are some of the best deals in town!

I highly recommend a stay in West Cape May at Eldredge House. The location is a quiet, relaxing setting away from the hustle and bustle of downtown Cape May, and early American history lovers can bathe in some of the peninsula's rich history—just make sure you check the bath tub first to make sure something else isn't already bathing!

As for the ghosts, they have probably been haunting this house for over 100 years. Very few people have even noticed them in all this time. If you happen to be psychic, or highly intuitive, you probably *will* notice them. If you do not possess psychic or intuitive abilities, you may only experience the ghosts of Eldredge House through these pages.

In either case, Eldredge House is a great place to stay and I, for one, will be back!

Now about those other ghostly children hanging around the old Eldredge property—let's take a walk back behind the Eldredge House to one of Todd's "newer" neighbors.

The Yellow House on Eldredge Avenue

BOY'S IN THE ATTIC—THE TYPE THAT HAUNT

Private Home - Eldredge Avenue West Cape May

I AM privileged to be able to meet so many great open-minded people at my lectures, dinners and book signings. I guess it's the subject matter that keeps most skeptics away. Barring a few bored husbands, who have been dragged by their wives to my events, and would much rather be back at home watching some game on TV, most of the people I meet and greet love the idea of ghosts and hauntings.

After one of my tours I got an email from a lady named Barbara Morgan. Barbara lived in West Cape May and asked if I would ever be interested in doing a walk-through of her home on Eldredge Avenue to check for ghosts. At the time of her email, the idea of a West Cape May Ghost Trolley Tour was just a distant fantasy. I was busy enough getting *Book 1* launched. As the years passed, Barbara kept bugging me to come to her house, and I finally relented in the fall of 2007.

As I mentioned in the introduction, West Cape May is not my normal stomping ground. Each time I get called to a new location to investigate for ghosts, I am amazed that I had never noticed the houses here before. Such is the life of a medium with ADD.

We dropped in on Barbara in early October of 2007. Willy and I sat with her in the living room of her early 20th century home on Eldredge Avenue, that just happened to be situated on a lot that at one time was part of the Eldredge property. In fact, she is practically in Todd Land's back yard!

The Yellow House on Eldredge Avenue

When Barbara first contacted me about the old home she and her husband Ron had purchased in July of 2006, she was not sure there was anything significant going on, but she wanted me to double check. She had felt something odd in one particular third floor room from the beginning, and had also sensed and heard a presence on the enclosed front porch, but saw nothing each time she got up to look.

As I mentioned earlier, I had been through several homes in West Cape May in 2006 and found little or no activity. From the incidents Barbara had described to me, I felt this was probably another one of those, excuse the pun, dead ends. How wrong I was!

I focused my energy on the living room, and then slowly let it expand until I felt I had enveloped the entire house. I began to detect an older woman, hunched over with a watering can, watering pots of geraniums. Her energy felt like it was coming from outside the house instead of inside.

Barbara told me that two sisters lived next door to her for many years, and it sounded like I was describing the sister who loved to garden — except she was still alive. I realized I was tapping into some sort of warp. It has happened before. I was once channeling for a friend's mother-in-law, years ago up here in north Jersey, and the same thing happened. All of these vivid images were coming through from the 1930s, and the people I was seeing in the past were still alive in the present.

I think psychic energy can go forward and backward. Since time is not linear, at least many metaphysically minded people do not think it is, then a person with psychic ability should be able to see a person's past events as well as their future events. For physical locations, I have found certain spots hold their past connection more strongly than others. This property seemed to have a strong residual charge.

I started to sense a doctor, retired I thought, walking around the space where the house now sat. There were several doctors who lived nearby, so this "could" have been a ghost or just another residual strand of energy. There were also images of horses and a feeling of a time long ago.

The most interesting thing happened next. I started getting a strong feeling of a man named "Harry." At the time, I did not know about Harry S. Eldredge, who I mentioned in the last chapter as drowning at sea and coming back to the Eldredge House. I only discovered that ghost in the Eldredge House after reviewing all of the tapes of the investigations. That fact had just come to light in March of 2008. I was visiting Barbara six months earlier. Since we were right in Todd's back yard, the ghosts from the Eldredge House most likely were either coming to see me or I had stumbled onto one of their outdoor activities?

Harry was a stronger presence and was showing me the property as it was when he was alive. He was showing me a well. There was none on Barbara's property that she knew of at the time. Todd Land did tell me that when he was digging in his back yard one day, he dug down and hit a brick floor that was quite expansive. He thought it may have been a barn floor from the past. It was near the property line between his house behind Barbara's. There could very well have been out buildings, but none of the old maps I have seen show them.

Barbara Morgan's house also shows up first on the Sanborn 1921 map. It is not on the 1890 Sanborn map. Historian Mike Conley felt the house was built somewhere between 1900–1920 after he did the historical survey on the building. The only thing that was not done is a title search on past owners of the house, so at this point we can not confirm if any of these names apply to her house or Todd's. Ghosts move around just like we living people do.

Next I sensed a young girl with blond curley hair showing up at the door. She was definitely a ghost. Barbara's cat, Che-Si, was prancing around the house at the time of my investigation and her greyhound, April, was darting back and forth watching me from afar. I was curious to see if they sensed anything. Usually cats are drawn to psychic energy, Barbara's cat was more interested in it's mouse toy under the couch. April was much more in tune. Go figure.

I was picking up more external house energy at this point. I started hearing horses again. I was not aware of any stables on the property, but a lot can change in almost 200 years.

"I hope you're not picking that up from me," Barbara interjected, "I'm a horse person, I ride a horse everyday," she added.

This might have been exactly what was happening. I might have been picking up Barbara's energy instead of the property's energy.

I sensed the name "Judy" or "Julie" then, "Madeleine." There was a Judith Eldredge and also a Judith Hughes, but I am not sure if they would have called either woman "Judy" in those days. These ghosts could also have been coming from surrounding houses. This has been happening more and more to me in Cape May. I must be getting a reputation!

Next we headed to the basement with Barbara. The heating unit was humming away in the background. If I had a comfortable chair and an hour, I could have let the white noise put me into a trance state. Then I could have psychically hooked into the time warp. Other than that idea, I was not sensing anything in particular in the cellar, so there was no need to stay. Footsteps could then be heard—walking above us. "The ghost?" I asked Barbara.

"My husband Ron," she replied, referring to her living husband who had just arrived home. After a quick "hello" to Ron, we followed Barbara up to the second floor. A lot of passers-by, I thought, but no strong ghost activity in the house. Then I entered one of the upstairs bedroom and my paranormal world just got a little brighter.

"I just walked through this door and I could feel someone in here. It's very strong," I told Barbara. "Before we walked in, this room felt occupied," I added.

It was young a boy, and I could read his thoughts at point blank range, yet I had not been able to sense him before this. Could changing our location in a building also move us into another part of the ghost realm? I turned a corner, and there he was. I had no sense of him being in the room beforehand. He was not in my psychic radar until I was practically on top of him. Their physical space does not correspond to ours.

I could see Andrew in my mind's eye. It was not a complete image, but enough to make out that it was a child, a boy of about seven or eight years of age. When Barbara entered the room, he smiled. I could sense his joy. He told me he stayed in that room because it was unoccupied. Barbara confirmed that fact.

Barbara Morgan just radiates sunshine. She is like a water cooler of positive energy! This young boy knew it as well, and that's why he moved in.

"He's not with the house," I told Barbara, "he came here because he likes you." Barbara seemed comfortable with that idea.

The little boy sat in the corner of the room, peering up at us. I remember his large eyes stood out in the psychic image he was projecting.

"Somethings's playing with me in this house, and I will tell you about it when we are all done," Barbara revealed.

"It's the ghost of a child. This is a young boy" I told her, "and I am getting the name Andrew."

"I just got chills up and down my arms when you said that name," Barbara exclaimed.

This is a reaction worth noting. Barbara already knew I was sensing a child. She even knew it was a young boy. I had revealed both of those things to her. It was not until I said the name of the child that she got "goose bumps" on her arms.

When a ghost comes into our space, we usually experience some sort of energy interaction. Symptoms may be a sudden chill, the hair standing up on our neck and arms, or plain old pins and needles or goose bumps. Goose bumps are usually caused by a physical sensation of being cold or a psychological reaction to fear.

In cases of ghost interaction fear is the main player, however recognition of something we know to be true on a subconscious level also may trigger this reaction.

I have seen this before when I reveal the true identity of someone's ghost to the person who has experienced or lived with it. It is exhilarating and relieving. The boy was sending me his identity on a psychic level and, because I am a practicing psychic medium, I recognize this communication and know how to interpret it. Barbara, on the other hand, is just an innocent bystander to a haunting. She is an unsuspecting participant, one could say. This house is a second home for Ron and Barbara. Because Barbara only moved into the house in July of 2006, I don't think she ever had the chance to make a complete connection with the ghost—at least while she was awake.

Most people who live with a ghost, either don't know it, or don't want to know it. There is a small percentage who want to know who or what is haunting their house, and that percentage is growing, but now, most people are in the dark about their household haunts.

Some people actually interact with ghosts in their dreams. These lucid dreams and conversations might feature people we have never met, yet we may form long-term friendships with these same ghosts in a dream state.

In other words, one might think he or she is just dreaming, when in fact they are really interacting with their ghosts on another level of consciousness. When we dream, we generally apply a suspension of disbelief. We usually do not recognize the people that we are interacting with as ghosts. Unless they become threatening or menacing and reveal their true identity in the dream. Not a nice feeling.

When we dream, ghosts appear to us as living people. They are usually not frightening at all. If it is a child's ghost that comes to you in a dream, most would recognize it only as a child. I think Andrew had made previous contact with Barbara; she just did not have any conscious memory of the interaction. When I brought his name to her conscious mind's attention, a connection may have been made. She definitely felt *something*, and I do not think it was fear.

So why don't these same ghosts communicate with all of us while we are awake? Why are they so antisocial? This is deliberate on the ghost's part—at least in the case of adult ghosts. They do not want to have a living companion. They are still attached to the living world for a reason known only to them. But as far as needing a friend to hang with, most are not interested in the idea. From what I can tell, ghosts would rather mix with other ghosts.

There is a communication gap between the living and the dead. A ghost will only expend so much energy trying to communicate with the living. Compare this to having neighbors who do not speak your language. You might try to communicate for a while, but if you still can not understand a word they are saying after a few weeks, you would probably give up on the idea of striking up a conversation.

A psychic medium is not always spot on. There are days when I just can't tap into the energy as there are ghosts who will not meet me half way. If you want to communicate, you gotta meet the neighbors at the fence.

Ghosts of children are different from ghosts of adults. They are needier, and long for companionship. Most of these children were deprived of their lives when they were under ten years of age. They try to create bonds to strong mother or father figures. Motherly figures like Barbara Morgan, who radiate sunshine and strong positive energy, must send these ghostly kids dashing off to the corner store to buy Mother's Day cards!

Andrew is definitely one of those kids.

I started to get shocks up both arms. I had struck a chord of truth. I told Andrew that I was running a tape, and if he had anything to say he should say it now. I would be able to play it back for Barbara later. He spoke, I didn't listen. I have to admit, I missed this one. I had scanned this tape, or so I thought, after I had uploaded it to my computer months ago. It was only when I was sitting at my desk, writing this book, that I picked up a response to my request on the tape.

A slow, deep voice speaks on the tape. EVPs never seem to come in at the correct speed. I compensate for this by raising or lowering the pitch, or increasing or decreasing the speed, until the voice sounds more natural.

It was a child's voice saying to Barbara, "My mother died." I sent the EVP off to Barbara right away. I listened to it repeatedly to make sure those were the words until I started to get teary-eyed. I don't think there is anything more heartbreaking than listening to a child say his mother died. No wonder he loves Barbara's energy. She probably reminds him of his real mother.

There is always a question of what to do with these young ghosts, and Barbara asked me that very question.

"I don't know," is usually my response to this question, "You can try to send them away. You can try, but it's like sending your kid out into the night alone and helpless."

I know there are higher Angelic beings that could help this child and other children cross over to Heaven, but all of these souls young and old, have free choice. I do not think anyone can force them to go against their will. At least that's how I perceive the way in which this higher power works. Maybe this is even part of those soul's natural path. Hopefully, some higher power is there waiting, in case these ghosts *do* want to leave.

Andrew continued to send me more psychic communications. He said he was afraid of clowns. I am not sure where he was seeing a clown, but one was scaring him. Great, clowns are creepy enough. Now I've got a scary *dead* clown hanging out in West Cape May!

Barbara had told me that Andrew's room was the last room that they had furnished. They had not been using it since they bought the house. He had apparently been in the house since Barbara and Ron had moved in. Barbara wondered if he was from the neighborhood, that perhaps there was an Andrew who died on the street years ago.

He gave me the feeling that he climbed up the house and looked in the bedroom window. The common misconception that ghosts fly through the air and pass through walls is all Hollywood and no fact. The ghosts I have encountered follow the same routes the living do. Ghosts do not pass through walls or solid matter. It's all doors and windows for them.

Andrew made a comment to me that, "Barbara was the nicest so far." I felt this meant that he favored her over the previous owners. Since he also entered the house via a window on the second floor, I could speculate that he did not belong to that house. Instead he died elsewhere or more likely, lived elsewhere in the neighborhood.

As we stood in the bedroom, an EVP appeared high in the white noise of the tape. I stripped the recording of all the static. A man's voice says, "Why are you standing? Sit down!"

It was not a child's voice this time, and I did not sense the ghost of a man in the room with us.

EVPs can be tricky things and, when comparing them to psychic evidence, one should proceed with caution.

With my mind, I can psychically pick up the thoughts and feelings of ghosts. I am technically mind reading.

The EVP recordings, theoretically, are recording ghost "voices" or telepathic signals, but how truthful are these messages?

A person can be thinking one thing and saying another. If I sense a ghost with the name of "Paul" and at the same time the EVP records, "Jack," which one do I take as fact?

If I am mind reading a ghost, so to speak, then even if the ghost is denying the information, the psychic communication will have a feeling of truthfulness. I have encountered these contradictions in ghost hunting before. Ghosts are capable of lying. People do it.

Think about it, a ghost does not want to be discovered, so they give a false name and it appears as an EVP. We may get so caught up in the amazement of actually capturing a ghost's voice on tape, we forget to check the legitimacy of the fact. I could say I was Benjamin Franklin on tape. That does not mean I really am Benjamin Franklin. Couldn't a ghost do the same? If a ghost tells me to "get out," or to "F--- off," then I have to look at any EVP evidence from that ghost as suspect.

When it comes to ghost hunting, it is all about parapsychology. It takes some degree of psychological detective work to figure out a ghost's true personality. I am *not* trained as a psychologist, by the way, but I do have a lot of experience dealing with people. I worked in retail for over 30 years!

I can sometimes get a good feeling if a ghost is not being truthful or giving me false information when I am channeling during an investigation. On the other hand, if my energy is diminished and my mind is not 100% focused, I may be misinterpreting the psychic information. This is why I try to be well rested for a ghost investigation or a channeling session with a client. Luckily, Andrew was a good soul and really wanted to talk to me and especially Barbara. He really had no reason to lie as she welcomed him to stay as long as he liked. He went on and on about all kinds of things. He was a typical gabby little kid, just dead.

Andrew loved boats, he said, and also complained about Barbara's dog "making stinkies."

"He did! Our old dog Niles, had terrible gas!" Barbara exclaimed. I guess ghosts can smell as well as they can hear. On the other hand, I have also felt they can access sensations that we, the living, are experiencing by tapping into our minds. Or he could simply have seen Barbara and Ron talking about their former dog's gas problem and was repeating it for our sake. It was hard to tell.

Barbara mentioned about her dog and cat going up to the third floor, turning around, and running back down. She also has had repeated problems with smoke detectors chirping as if their batteries were low, except the batteries are changed and the chirping continues.

I made my way up to the third floor and could immediately sense a strong energy in one of the rooms. I could still feel Andrew's energy radiating upward, perhaps he even followed me, but I was not aware he did at the time.

"This side has the energy," I told Barbara, referring to one of the bedrooms. "This room is very active," I added.

"My cat actually did come to the third floor and I followed her to see what she would do. She poked her head in and meowed, turned around and rushed down." Barbara's animals rarely go to the third floor without her anymore. It seems they get spooked by the energy. "They (the cat and dog) won't come in these two rooms," she added as I felt my way around the third floor bedroom.

Barbara also thought the rooms drain energy. The smoke detectors are hard-wired, also run on batteries and the batteries are constantly going dead. She also sent me a picture recently where the smoke detector looked as if it had been yanked from the ceiling!

The room's energy began to affect all of us. Willy started to feel dizzy, and I could sense a barrage of energy, like a time warp from multiple years all converging at once. The name "Kenny" popped into my head. At a point right after that on the tape I ask, "Is this the room that you like to stay in?"

"Eddy," is the response given by a young man. Was I psychically hearing "Kenny," yet it was really "Eddy" who was in the room with us? Those two names are close enough in sound that a thought wave or sound wave could get slightly corrupted and cause them to sound differently.

I next sensed an old, grandfather-like figure. He was lamenting that his granddaughters had all died. He was crying out to us. The chaotic nature of the room suddenly began to make sense now, as I closed my eyes and listened to that part of the tape. The psychic energy was being radiated by several ghosts in the same space and the Grandfather figure was not focused, and was very agitated, as if he was having trouble remembering things. It seemed like he had dementia. That dementia-like state was permeating the ethers of the room and creating chaotic strings of thoughts going off on tangents in all directions. I felt like I had suddenly stepped inside the mind of someone suffering from failing mental ability.

There are bits and pieces of an older man talking on the tape. It is just rambling and does not make any sense. These background conversations often pop up on my tapes, and I keep trying to find a scientific explanation for them. It would be easy to discount them if it was provable that radio, television or cell phone signals were being picked up on my tape recorder, but as far as I know, those signals are mostly digital now and the cassette recorder is analog. Anyway, these EVPs do not sound like a telephone conversation or a radio broadcast. EVPs are typically choppy bits of dialogue, some of which makes no sense at all. So, until someone discovers otherwise, we will continue to assume that these phantom voices are the disembodied souls that we call ghosts and that they have found a way to imprint their thoughts/voices on my tape.

"Let's move back down," I told Barbara, "the energy in this room is too heavy." Either a warp in time is running through that part of the house, or Barbara is lodging a ghostly family on the third floor! It's not a bad feeling, just a heavy feeling that started to drain me.

The EVPs up on the third floor were in the white noise and had to be "exhumed" from the static. As we made our way back down to the second floor and into Andrew's room, the EVPs went from a faint Class C to an audible Class A.

"We're back in Andrew's room now," I stated for the record.

"Who is asking for me?" replied a voice on he tape, this time older sounding than before. Had he aged significantly in the last 30 minutes? It was strange to hear a different voice. EVPs can distort and morph, but this was weird.

After we spent a few more minutes in Andrew's room we headed down to the living room to wrap up the investigation, which was much more than I had expected when we first drove up to the house. I told Barbara the best thing to do is just live in peace with the ghosts. They were there first after all. She agreed and seemed comfortable with all of the new information I had brought to light.

Since my initial visit in October 2007, Barbara has come to terms with her unseen guests. She even put a little boat in Andrew's room, since Andrew told us he loved ships. Andrew seems to like the new attention. Barbara has told me she even senses him out on the porch sometimes. He is a strong, but benevolent spirit. Like having a child living in the house, without all the added noise.

Ghost Lesson Number 1 — peaceful coexistence is the best policy. The house is calm now and everyone there seems at peace. Well, almost—

As for the chirping smoke detectors, which start and then stop as soon as Barbara goes to investigate (and it always happens when she is alone in the house) she finally figured out the solution.

"I just went out the front door and yelled back to them, 'knock it off!' You know when you notice something because all of a sudden it isn't there? When I came back inside the house, the chirping had completely stopped."

Ghost Lesson Number 2 — always start by asking nicely. Then when you have had enough of their antics should they be playing with you — you are allowed to vent.

The yellow house on Eldredge Avenue is just one of many old houses in West Cape May with extra tenants. These unseen visitors may stay for a few months or a few years. It all depends on how well they like the house and the host or hostess. Barbara definitely is a hit on the ghost circuit, at least with a little boy named Andrew. At least there is one less orphaned child-ghost in Cape May now. Hey, there's an idea, a ghost adoption agency! What *would* the neighbors think!

Why don't we find out by visiting another one of Barbara's neighbors across the road.

Wait, that house is haunted also! Oh, well. You are in good company in West Cape May, Barbara!

Flanegan Art & Framing
DEATH IMITATES ART
324 North Broadway, West Cape May

THE first person I went to see on my quest to find the other ghosts of West Cape May was Diane Flanegan. Diane and her husband Rich own Flanegan Art & Framing. Diane was the one who graciously guided me to The Eldredge House, and spent most of the first day of our investigation with us. When we were done at Todd Land's Eldredge House, we made our way back across Broadway to the Flanegan's to see if they had any ghostly guests. As I crossed the road, I looked up at the old home and thought, for just a second, someone was watching us from the very top attic window. Maybe it was just a trick of the light playing against the old Gothic window in the gable of the house, or maybe the ghosts knew they were next.

The Flanegans have now set up their art studio and framing business on the first floor of their circa 1880s Victorian at 324 Broadway, on the corner of Fourth Avenue. A few years ago, they rented out their house as the "Dorothy May Guest Suites," and at that time I had tried to get in to investigate, but was unable to do so. I had heard stories of the house being haunted, but West Cape May seemed like another world and, sadly, I never pursued the ghosts there — until now.

Diane and Rich live in the house full time now so I was able to do a complete psychic sweep of the premises. When I stepped through the front door of the art and frame shop, the first thing I felt was not paranormal energy, it was *creative* energy. That energy actually has a different feeling, and this shop was *buzzing* with art and art energy. Both Diane and Rich are accomplished artists and, if you love art, definitely stop by to see their shop.

There was actually so much of Rich and Diane's energy in the shop, I could not get a fix on anything paranormal. Once I walked back into their living room, however, I felt the entire energy change. Unseen forces were around me, and they were quite settled in at the old house.

Gerry Eisenhaur was along with us, with his ghost hunting equipment in tow. I can always tell by Gerry's reaction to a new haunt that he has a hidden psychic ability. A strong haunt hits him like a ton of bricks. Many intuitives will experience becoming slightly dizzy, or even nauseous, when they first set foot in a haunted place. Once psychic people get used to the energies, equilibriums return to normal. They still may feel drained by the ordeal.

The distinction I make, by the way, between psychics and intuitives is, that psychics have developed their intuitive powers and know how to deal with the information coming into their minds. Whereas intuitive people may feel or sense the things that a psychic feels, they do not always know what to do with that information. Intuitives are ordinary people. They possess varying degrees of empathic abilities. Psychics are more fully charged with ability and may use this gift in some form of professional capacity.

It did not take my brain very long to latch on to a lady ghost in the house. As I looked around the living room, I heard the woman make a comment that the fireplace was missing. The Flanegan's had a fireplace in the room, but it was fake. Rich said he would have to check behind the walls to find the real chimney.

With that Willy noticed a strange light around me. "There's a light near your hand," he said as the odd glow came and went.

"My EMF meter is starting to jump," Gerry added.

The room was warming up for a show. My cassette tape recorder went on and off, but I was not touching the buttons. Something was either inspecting us or the close proximity of the ghost's energy was colliding with our energy. The same thing seems to happen to lights, televisions, and anything else of an electric nature. Either ghosts deliberately manipulate these things or their energy inadvertently sets them off.

Gerry scanned the room. Diane's living room chair sent the EMF meter jumping. *Something* was sitting in the chair. I moved over and placed my hand in the space. I received a name like "hill". I continued to check the room and moved out to the side porch and kitchen. There was very little energy in that area, almost none. Diane told me that section was added in the 1930s and was not part of the original house. Some ghosts may stick to their old house plan and not venture into a newer section if they think it does not belong to them. Ghosts feel what was theirs in life is still theirs in death but, in my experience, they usually do not claim more than the original space. This applies to ghosts haunting their own homes. There are exceptions to every rule when it comes to the paranormal. Generally though, old ghosts follow old paths and habits.

I was next given the name "Ruth." Diane knew no Ruth who had owned the house. Later during the Highland House investigation a Ruth was listed on the deed list. That would have been a stretch, since Highland House was a distance down the road. I am sure there was a closer Ruth at one time in history, but we have no record of her at this time.

The name "Tom" and "Mary" also came through next. As if a group of ghosts were gathering to see what I would find, or more likely, if I could find *them*. Over the next year, while working on The Eldredge House investigation across the street, I found that Thomas Eldredge owned that house (see the previous chapter on the Eldredge House) and it was built on his Aunt Mary Eldredges property. Could this have been the Tom and Mary? They are common names, but the proximity to he house across the street, which I had not yet been in to see, made this information a little more applicable.

Diane and Rich told me the house was built in 1875, however it was not on the Swain's 1877 map. I emailed Mike Conley as I was writing this chapter, and he said that the house was shown as the W. Eldredge House on the 1886 Map, but it did not appear on the 1872

Beers Map. So it is more likely the house was built in the late 1870s. I also found it fascinating, but not surprising, that the house was originally an Eldredge house. The Flanegans had heard Annie Hand was the second owner. Annie's granddaughter Isabella, who had just died prior to my investigation, had given them that information.

"I keep hearing that the television turns on and off, by itself, like she has been doing that here," I told the Flanegans.

"She used to," Diane said.

"With the last set, not this one," Rich added.

As I said, ghosts can affect anything electrical. Have a ghost? You will never need a remote!

I asked the woman to elaborate about turning on and off the television. She promptly denied having anything to do with it. It was "before her time," she said. The woman blamed the ghost of a young boy. The imagery I received as she told me about the boy was that he fell through ice and drowned. Apparently, the boy had been playing with the television, and she told me he was also fond of the Flanegan's dog, Mocha, who by the way, had a tail that could be used as a whip!

The name "Ruth" popped into my head again. I tried to verify if they were actually saying "route" instead, but the only route she commented on was her milkman's — and he was dead. Great, more dead children and now dead milkmen! Wasn't that a band?

The EMF field jumped to 0.9 from 0.2. It kept flip flopping, when it should have remained stationary. Gerry discovered, with his meters, that there was a power line running to the ceiling fan. Even if it was reading the power lines, it should not have been fluctuating as if it were sitting stationary on the coffee table.

We also watched the EMF meter move up and down when it was placed on the chair. I thought it was about time that damn thing finally did something. I gave my EMF meter away years ago to Diane Bixler. Diane runs the Haunted Cape May walking tour and I thought she would get better use out of it, as a show and tell. If I remember correctly, I think she had about as much success with it as I did. Luckily, Gerry seems to have a knack for electronic equipment. The meter seems to like him!

The ghostly woman felt very much at home in the room she called the "parlor." She kept tabs on all the comings and goings and mentioned Diane baking and also burning something awful on the stove. Diane told us she had been melting glass on the stove and it stunk up the house. The chair in the "parlor" seemed to be her favorite spot to sit. She was no longer a fan of the Flanegan's couch, as she referred to it as "the inquisition!"

"I hate that couch!" Diane said. She agreed with the ghost. It was, apparently, uncomfortable enough to bother even those without bodies!

The female presence gave me the name "Anna." I mentioned the name to Diane and Rich.

"Annie Hand. We know that she used to live here for a long time," Diane recalled. This piece of information felt right. It just psychically fit into place.

Annie asked if she would be thrown out of her home. This is a common fear that most of the ghostly inhabitants in town seem to share, at least the ones that I have encountered that will communicate with me. The Flanegans assured her she could stay as long as she liked.

Annie was not ready to move on just yet. She said people before the Flanegans had tried to throw her out

"We are not going to throw her out. She was here before we were," Diane reassured her unseen friend.

Annie seemed relieved.

She also asked me if she was going to be "part of a show?" I explained to her that it was a trolley tour that would be pivoting at her corner each night in the summer. This ghost had such a warm, down to earth feeling that I could have closed my eyes and thought I was talking with a living person in the room. The conversation was very casual and relaxed. Annie said others have seen and heard her over the years, that she hums or sings to herself.

Ghosts are social creatures, not isolationists. They socially interact, and where I find one, I usually find two or more. Annie lamented that the neighborhood had changed. The dead had been moving out; her friends were gone now. Her old ghostly friends had stayed for a while, but eventually crossed over to Heaven. There was a note of sadness in her voice when she told me this. It was not verbal, I was hearing her voice with my mind, but with the messages came various feelings and this time she felt sad.

From what I have heard from the ghosts, it seems that many have made stop-overs on the ghost plane before they moved on to Heaven. We all seem to have business to get in order before we go on. There are so many unresolved things to take care of before we die. We just run out of time and have to pick up the pieces of our life as ghosts. Such is death.

This was a good house for EVP energy as well. During my conversation with the Flanegans, there were a continuous sound of women talking on the tape . Was this Annie and the ghost who called herself Ruth? The voices were not directed at me. They were very faint and in the background noise. There were no explainable outside sources for this noise, no radios or television were on in the house, and we were the only ones present.

Annie Hand commented on the artwork being done in the gallery. She said she has been sending creative energy to the Flanegans over the past several months. Rich and Diane said they had been feeling inspired with their art recently. Maybe Annie had started the creative flow! I feel creative energy *is* channeled from a higher source. Writing, composing, painting and acting are all using creative channeled energies. This might be a form of psychic communication that higher beings send to us.

Annie kept mentioning having her portrait painted and, since Rich was the painter in the family, he could do the job. I am not sure if this ever happened Rich was intrigued by the idea and the descriptions I had given him of Annie. He thought she could help him paint an accurate portrait. As we moved from room to room, the energy flowed with us. Could the ghosts be basking in this creative energy, channeled over the years by the Flanegans artistry? I found the idea of ghosts influencing art fascinating. I wonder how often we are influenced by our unseen friends? I feel I was motivated to write when I stayed in some of the old B&Bs in Cape May. I always chalked this up to ambience, maybe it truly *was* ghost writing!

We followed Diane and Rich up the stairs to the second floor. The energy got more intense. I tried to stay focused. My ADD taking over my mind one minute and a ghost taking over my mind the next—just another day at work for me.

Annie talked. I channeled. The Flanegans listened. Gerry's camera batteries started to drain. Something was suddenly tugging at our energy, as we arrived on the second floor side porch. This area was now a laundry room with a small bathroom attached. It also felt *extremely* haunted.

"At one time, there was a very long, seven foot, wrought iron bathtub in here. One of the Hands, the father, was a huge man, I was told."

Diane pointed to where the old tub used to be and I started receiving a frenzy of psychic images. It was like standing in a dark room with mimes trying to attack you, while a strobe light flashed!

Diane was talking, but I was starting to lose it. I felt dizzy like I was falling. "This used to be a bathroom —we think this was an addition to the original house."

I tried to maintain the conversation, but it was proving difficult as the room was having a strange affect on me. Something unpleasant had happened in there, but I was not sure what it was. Unfortunately, the person it happened to was standing *right in front of me!*

The batteries were getting zapped and something was in that room with us. A strange sound appears in a spot in the tape when I stopped speaking. I thought it was me exhaling, but when I sped up the recording it became a child saying, "Let me up," and the sound of *water bubbling*. Could a child have accidently drowned in the old iron tub in the early days of the house?

Annie told us, through me, that she did not go in that room. She gets vertigo. I knew what she meant. I walked into the adjoining bathroom but the feeling did not get any better. The sink was dripping and the drips seemed to take on a piercing sound in my head.

Children's voices were popping up on the tape at this point. A child said, "I can't run" while the other exclaimed, "Let me talk to them." The EVP was very high pitched and I had to slow the speed to hear what they were saying. The sound waves must have been coming in fast. I also noticed the tape I was using was making a constant *click-click* sound. This sound was actually *enhancing* the EVPs. The same thing was happening in the living room when a car was heard driving by. The EVPs would momentarily get louder with the car noise. I think this lends credibility to the theory that EVPs are manipulated sound. The ghosts take an existing sound and piggyback their own sounds or words on these carrier waves. It seems like that is what was happening here at least.

Haunted plumbing? The old porch bathroom and laundry room at the Flanegan home is one of the most hopping haunts in town!

What could have happened in this room, I thought? Was there an accident? A death in the old iron tub? Or was the ghost just being dramatic to try to scare me? They may do this to get someone to leave.

"I am hearing the name Thomas again," I told the group. Right after I say that, on the tape, a clear EVP says, "I'm Ann." I guess Annie thought I was confusing her with someone else!

When I first reviewed the Flanegan tapes last spring, there was an incredible EVP right near this point in the tape. I pause for a second, on the tape while we are talking about the porch originally being one large bathroom. A child's laughter can be heard right after I stop talking. I was so amazed I copied the segment to use later in my lectures. Then, something strange happened. I reviewed the same tape a day later, and the child's laughter was missing from the segment! Thinking I had lost my place, I brought up the copy of the clip on my computer. The child's laughter was missing from *that* version as well!

Equilibrium takes a holiday in the old bathroom on the second floor of the Flanegan's house — the ghostly energy puts a new spin on things!

How could an EVP vanish from of two separate copies of a recording? It only happened that one time and so far, thankfully, it has not happened since. I cannot explain it at all, but then again, I can also not explain what the heck EVPs are either, so it is par for the course!

The old bathroom turned sun porch, turned laundry room with a bathroom, was really a head trip. This has to be one of the most haunted rooms in Cape May! I am not sure what happened in that room to cause a child's ghost to become attached to it. The room is just *very* active paranormally. It ranks right up with the best haunts in town!

I told Diane and Rich that I sensed a person who drowned in the tub. He or she may have had epilepsy or something similar and had a seizure while bathing. It did not occur to me at the time of the investigation, but later I realized that the ghost of the boy downstairs might not have fallen through ice and drowned, he may have slipped in the tub, hit his head and then drowned.

The EVPs of a child talking were prevalent in that upstairs porch area where the child's energy saturated the room. Gerry's equipment jumped with the energy. A circuit panel in the room, was also throwing off EMF energy, as was a refrigerator nearby.

Were the ghosts using all of this excess EMF as fuel? Historically, in paranormal research/ghost hunting, there has been a correlation between high EMF readings and haunting activity. Where there is a high EMF source in a haunted house, there is usually paranormal activity. Got a haunted room? Check where the power lines come into the house or where they run behind the walls of a room. They usually match locations of heavier haunting activity.

I was not alone in my experience of an uneasy feeling in the porch and bathroom area. When the Flanegans were having the bathroom repaired, the plumber also had a disturbing encounter.

"He was working in the bathroom when he saw the door start to close slowly. Instead of it stopping at the middle, it went all the way through to the other side! He packed up his tools and rushed out of the house and he has never been back since," Diane told us.

All of the EVPs I captured on cassette tape, in that bathroom area, sounded like someone talking under water. Non of the other investigation tapes had sounded like this.

A child says, "I will die there." I think, gesturing to someone where the tub had been.

Next an adult male replies, "So let's die then, and move on."

Was someone trying to get the boy to cross over to Heaven? Had I captured a guardian spirit on tape trying to help the child or was it just another male ghost in the house?

As I started probing around the room another EVP says, "Get out!" Serves me right for disturbing someone's bath.

Diane told me they had been speaking with an older woman who had lived in West Cape May her entire life. After the plumber incident in the bathroom, she thought to ask the woman if she knew if anything had happened in that room. The woman told her that yes, something did happen, but she could not talk about it because she knew the family. Damn! So close to finding out the true story! This made me think that the tragedy might have been more recent. We do not know when the iron tub was finally removed. Perhaps in time the little boy in the tub will be revealed. Maybe the spirit guides will help him cross over before that time, or maybe he just likes to hang out at the Flanegans. Ghosts are attracted to positive energy, and ghosts of children hunger for the family setting that they lost.

We walked through the rest of the house, but the paranormal energy was zero. I noticed on the tape there was a complete absence of EVP activity everywhere but downstairs in the living room and on the second floor on the porch. The hauntings were very localized in this house. When we were in the parlor the first time, the temperature reading on the chair was the same as the rest of the room. Now it was four degrees colder. Annie must have been waiting for us!

The Flanegans did not experience much themselves, which is typical when you live in a haunted house for a while. The paranormal energy begins to mesh with the rest of the house energy and eventually goes unnoticed by the current living occupants. However, people who stayed at the house for short periods of time had a different experience.

Diane told us when her house was called the Dorothy May Guest Suites, they lived in the cottage and rented out the rooms in the house during the season.

When the house was rented out as guest suites on a weekly basis, the ghosts seemed to feel put out. The house had been divided up into two apartments at one point.

"We had a lot of comments when the place was guest suites, upstairs and down by people who would report strange things... doors opening and closing... strange things," Rich recalled.

"She was very unhappy when there were people coming weekly. We had a lot of activity, not just her, that's when the others were here too," Diane told us. The activity has quieted down quite a bit since the days when the Flanegans rented the house as suites. The ghosts seem much happier now. Ghosts, like living people, eventually get worn out by non-stop company!

"Up in that bathroom... people would come and tell us about what had happened the night before... they did not know each other — we didn't tape record it at the time. There was also a consistent story that there was a (ghost) dog on the property... a lot of people said they had seen a dog."

I did not sense a dog at all. Apparently the phantom dog had wandered off somewhere else. The Flanegans received numerous reports over the years of people afraid of the dog roaming the property. At the time, they did not have a dog and had never seen one around.

We sat in the living room to wrap up the investigation. I was asking the Flanegans a few last questions about their experiences with the ghosts during the time they rented the guest suites. Suddenly, something brushed the back of my head. It felt like a hand, giving me a loving touch like a "thank you." Pins and needles followed the feeling all over my head. I cannot remember any physical contact with a ghost being as strong as that day. No living person was near me at the time. It really felt like a hand. I guess in a sense it was — an Annie Hand, possibly expressing her gratitude for me acting as her interpreter.

"Annie is the strongest, and she is right in this room with us," I told Rich and Diane. She was the lady of the house, and I was not sure if she was connected with the boy upstairs or not. She was happy to be finally recognized. She stopped talking after that. Annie was content.

Was this Annie Hand haunting the house? The Flanegans told me she had sold the house in 1945 to Allen and Alberta Hand. They sold the house in 1971 to the people the Flanegans bought it from in 1997.

I did some genealogical detective work to find out more about the Hands. Annie Bishop was married to Milton Hand. Annie ran the Dry Goods store. She had two sons from a previous marriage, Garner and Leslie Bishop. I spoke with the charming, walking history book, Janet Eldredge Vance. Janet recalled Garner had helped his mother with the Dry Goods store. Walt Campbell also remembered Annie and her sons and feels the store may have been the building where Weddings by the Sea now resides.

Jim Campbell was able to locate everyone in Cold Spring Cemetery — everyone except Annie. There is no record of her being buried in the family plot, which I thought was odd, but she was remarried and maybe is with her first husband. Was it Annie Bishop Hand who was still watching over her old home? So far, no other "Ann" has turned up connected with 324 N. Broadway. Allen Hand, who bought the house from Annie was a second cousin of Milton Hand. He raised his three daughters in the house, Emily, Hope and Joyce, who have all now passed, so I could not interview them about the home's history.

There is always a chance that another Ann may have lived in the house. The ghost gave me no clues about herself or her family. She discussed matters of the house, not matters of the heart. In this respect, she seemed a more private person. I am making the assumption that is was Annie Hand that we were in contact with at the time. The name Thomas kept repeating in the bathroom, so the boy may be Thomas. The original owner of the Flanegan's house was William Eldredge and he was either the son or grandson of Enoch Eldredge. Since Enoch had purchased most of his sibling's land across the street after his mother Judith had died, he may have purchased land on the other side of the street as well.

Diane emailed me today to tell me that Daniel and Hattie Stevens also owned the house before the Hands. She thought the name Hattie was an interesting coincidence, because the name Hattie was also scratched into Todd's widow across the street at Eldredge House.

"Not a coincidence at all!" I wrote her back.

Hattie Stevens and Harriet Sawyer Eldredge (1861-1904) were one and the same person. She was indeed the child who scratched her name in her old bedroom window, across the street at her father Thomas' house! In 1880, Hattie married Daniel Ezekiel Stevens (1857-1937.) The Stevens lived in Hattie's parents' home (Eldredge House) across the street with her parents and younger siblings, until they could get a house of their own. They moved across the street into William Eldredge's home, sometime in the 1880s. At some point they left that home and moved next door. The Hand family then bought their old house.

Daniel and Hattie had two children, Ida Eldredge Stevens (1884-1968) and Harry T. Stevens. Harry seems to disappear in the 1890s.

Harriet (Hattie) Eldredge Stevens' eternal signature etched in the glass window of her old childhood bedroom at Eldredge House — seen against a backdrop of her future home, built by her Uncle William Eldredge, across the street on Broadway.

Either he moved away, or he died. After Hattie died in 1904, Daniel re-married a woman named Sadie. Jim Campbell had no record of Harry, and I cannot find anything about what happened to him — but I am still looking. Could this be the child that died in the house? Could that be the reason the Stevens sold the house and moved next door?

A house full of ghosts, and mysteries — typical Cape May real estate! There is great energy here and ghosts that have stories to tell.

If a house could paint itself, this would be that house. You could bathe in the creative energy (Just don't use the second floor tub, it's occupied.)

I would highly recommend a visit to Flanegan Art & Framing. You will be dazzled by the art, and if you are lucky, the ghosts as well. West Cape May has a lot of great places to see. At Flanegans, there is always *something* exciting to see or some wonderful art being created — just don't forget to bring your own disappearing ink — it's in vogue!

The Old Reeves Homestead
THE LITTLE GIRL IN THE ATTIC
AND THE CAPTAIN IN THE MIRROR

Private Residence — 103 Stevens Street, West Cape May

I typically request additional information from homeowners after completing a ghost investigation of their properties. I follow up with questions about the structure's history or anything I might have forgotten to ask—while my ADD personality was bulldozing through the initial investigation. I may even request old pictures or historic photographs the owners may have in their possession, to add to the story if it will be going into one of my books.

I had emailed Beth Bozzelli, the current owner of the old Reeves home on Stevens and Sunset and asked if she had any pictures of her house that dated back to the 1800s. She responded, saying she would search through some of the county records for pictures. Imagine my delight, when I received an email entitled "Old House Pictures" from Beth, a few nights later at 10:32 PM. Opening the email revealed nothing but a blank screen. No message and, sadly, no pictures. I was disappointed, but I emailed her back that there must have been some mistake when she tried to attach the files. A few minutes later, I received an email response telling me her account was over quota and the message had been delayed.

The next morning I left a message on her home phone about the problem with the email the night before. After I called her, I saw two more emailed had come in later that night—much later actually. The first emails came in at 1:47 AM, and the second rolled in at 3:02 AM. She must really be a night owl, I thought! But, she did follow up with the pictures and that was all I really cared about. I needed to get her chapter done and the book to the printer—wait a minute—the emails were empty again! Not even a text response. I called Beth on her cell phone this time, and updated her that she was using invisible ink on the emails!

A few days later, there was a message from Beth on my office telephone. She was surprised to hear that I was receiving emails from her since she had been on vacation in Antigua, and had just rushed home to Pennsylvania, to see her mother, who had fallen. To make matters even stranger, her computer was in Cape May, locked up in the house, where even the realtor could not get in while she was gone because the front storm door had been accidently locked.

Her laptop was sitting on her desk and it was turned on, but she was hundreds of miles away, and no one was home to respond to my emails.

Well, *something* was home, and that something apparently knows how to use a computer and send emails. This could only happen in Cape May!

The Old Reeves Homestead

The Reeves Homestead is one of my favorite houses in Cape May. It has sat on the corner of Sunset Boulevard and Stevens Street, possibly as far back as the 1830s. Each time I return from Cape May point I admire this beautiful old historic home, and dream about one day owning something just like it in Cape May.

My first experience with the Reeves Homestead was back in 2004, when my friends, Bob and Lisa Ransom owned the house. Lisa had invited Willy and me to stop over one night to meet her sisters and see what spirits may be hanging in the rafters. Luckily for me, the Baileys Irish Cream I was served was not the only spirit in the house that evening, but it *was* delicious.

As I talked with Lisa and her siblings, I could feel all kinds of energy in the house. I had noticed lights in the house and outside by the apartment addition would come on and go off by themselves. Timers, I wondered?

Lisa brought me over to living room closet under the stairs going to the second floor. She pointed to the old wood plank floor below and told me to look closely. I could see the boards had been very carefully cut to allow a section of the floor to be removed. A trap door?

"I have never opened it up," I remember Lisa saying that night.

I was dying of curiosity, but having forgotten my hammer and crowbar, I was not about to go digging. My first thought was "underground railroad." However, since that time, I have encountered some resistance from historians to the notion that Cape May was part of the network.

Harriet Tubman worked in Cape May as a cook and laborer in the early 1850s. She was on her way back from Canada and she worked in Cape May and Philadelphia during that period to earn money for her missions. In late 1852, she left Cape May to journey to Maryland to free her husband, John Tubman, and bring him back to safety in the north. But, when she snuck back to Maryland to rescue him, she found he had left her and married another woman — doesn't that suck. Tubman was a great lady, however. She turned the occasion into an opportunity, rescued a group of slaves instead and brought them to safety. Some historians say the Underground Railway did not cross the Delaware Bay, that it crossed instead the river up north by Camden. Others will argue that when Tubman worked in Cape May, she also set up a base here and brought slaves across the Delaware Bay to let them rest on the peninsula, before they headed north to Canada. I have heard various stories, and the only one that seems correct is that no one really knows what she did in Cape May.

Was Captain John Reeves sympathetic to the cause? Did he give Tubman's fugitive slaves refuge in a secret cellar in his old home? It is intriguing to think so. It is also intriguing to think about all of the history this old house has witnessed — and even more intriguing that some of those witnesses are still on hand!

Captain John W. Reeves (1840-1925) was a member of the large Reeves family and a Civil War veteran. The Reeves, like the Eldredges, populated much of West Cape May in the old days. Reeves seems to have lived in this home most of his adult life with his wife and three sons.

Jim Campbell had did a lot of research on the Reeves family at one point for the Greater Cape May Historical Society. He even found a picture of the Captain in his later years (pictured right) sitting with a group of Civil War Veterans. Jim had copied the picture from the Cape May County Museum a few years ago, but when he went back to make a better copy, the picture had been stolen. This has happened to so much historical material in Cape May. It is very sad as it is a loss for future generations of history lovers.

Jim sent me a copy of the picture he made of an old photograph of Captain John Reeves years ago. It was so grainy, I thought I could never use it. Then I looked at it again in the layout and thought, you know the old chap looks nice and ghostly as a copy of a copy!

A few years after my first visit, while I was scripting the West Cape May-Lighthouse ghost tour, I started thinking about Lisa and Bob's old home. They had since sold it and it was up for sale again. At first I decided not to bother the new owner. I was not sure if she knew the house was haunted, and I did not want to be the one to break the news to her! One afternoon, while sitting with Todd Land at The Eldredge House, I mentioned the Reeves Homestead.

"Oh, that's my friend Beth. She's great! She was the witch at our house on Halloween, and the kids loved her!" Todd told me. He called Beth on the phone, and she said she would love to have me come in and check out her home — and she said she *did* have activity!

It took a few months, but Willy, my friend Sandy (Gerry's Mom,) her daughter Jilly and I finally got over to her home this past February. We met Beth in her living room and she started to tell us some of her experiences. It seems she had found out the house was haunted as she was in the process of buying it, but she was fine with the idea and moved in with an open heart and open mind.

When I reviewed the tape of the investigation to write this chapter, I thought I had hit an EVP mother load! A woman's voice was singing in the background! I was amazed — until I realized Beth had left the radio on in the next room, which I eventually asked her to turn off. Sigh.

One of Beth's first experiences in her new home was one evening when she was sitting in the living room. It seems someone was watching her sitting on the couch and that someone — was *in* the mirror!

"I was sitting right here — I thought, because it was just a split second — I thought I was catching a glimpse of somebody (in the room) here," Beth said, as she gestured to the mirror across the room from where she had been sitting on the couch. At first, she thought there was a live person standing in the dining room and that she was seeing his reflection in the mirror in the living room. However when she turned to look, there was no one in the house but her and the mirror was now empty as well. She said it all happened in a split second.

Her description of the man looked very much like the picture Jim had given me of John W. Reeves, only a few years younger.

"I would describe him as a light-skinned person with a brown beard and longish brown hair — the beard was not a trimmed beard — it was just like scraggly here and came down — He was, I would say maybe in his thirties? I don't know. He had on a white shirt with a banded collar top — with buttons that came up to (the neck) and a brown jacket or a dark jacket."

I received the picture from Jim Campbell, after the investigation had taken place, so neither Beth nor I had ever seen a picture of John Reeves. Even with the graininess of the picture, Beth recognized the man could have been the same person, just shown to her as a younger man.

When I channel souls from the Other Side, especially ghosts, they may come through to me as they looked when they crossed over, but they also may appear much younger than they were when they died. I am not sure how a soul can recreate their earthly appearance, but if I could, I would surely pick a younger and slimmer me!

While historians have dated the house to around 1850, Beth found documentation tracing the house back to about 1837. Many of the old homes in Cape May started out as smaller dwellings and were expanded over the years. From the pattern of haunting activity in the house, I could get an idea that the ghosts were old and probably associated with the beginning of the house's history.

"It seems like anything that we sense is in the old part of the house. It's this bedroom, that's my son's bedroom, it's this part of the dining room," Beth told us as she described the oldest section of the house as being the living room, the dining room, and the downstairs bedroom where her son sleeps. None of the haunting activity takes place in the new addition, the new kitchen or any section that was added onto the original house. Once again, ghosts were following their original paths. This brings up the question again of what do they see? Are they seeing the way things were when they were alive? Can they see other souls, either living or dead? Do they transcend the earthly concept of time? Theories abound!

The ghosts did not take long to let Beth and her family know they were not alone in the old house. Her dogs would not cross the threshold of the doorway when they first arrived at their new home. They eventually coaxed them inside. Her daughters had an even better scare!

"Something happened when my two daughters were here. Scott and I were at the Phillies game. My two daughters, at that time maybe 21 and 17, were home. I got a hysterical call from my daughter saying, 'Mom, the doorknob to Sam's bedroom fell off!' I keep the door closed. I try not to go over this with my kids because they really don't want to stay in here by themselves. That scared them, and it scared me to the point because we were newly in the house. We hadn't even been here a full year."

The old white porcelain doorknob at the foot of the staircase leading upstairs stands out against the dark wood door like an antique porcelain doll in a thunderstorm. (Isn't that a scary image!) When I looked at the door from across the room, I even got a chill, thinking about watching it twist and turn, creaking along the way until finally, it popped out—and fell to the floor. No wonder her daughters went screaming out of the house and stayed in the car until she got home!

Once I got the wonderful Hollywood B Movie imagery out of everyone's minds (and you all know you love when stuff like this happens!) I explained what I thought *really* occurred.

It was a ghost doing the work. I sensed the ghost of a child—yes, yet another dead child haunting Cape May, surprise, surprise. This child was trying to get in to the bedroom where Beth's son was sleeping. I sensed the child liked the room because of things it found inside. Beth told me she had been keeping the door closed to that room

Opposite: The old porcelain doorknob that turned by itself and then fell off. Was something trying to get into the room—or out? (Photo by Sandra Bemis)

and if the ghost was following old paths, it needed to open the door to get through. Ghosts do open and close doors. They cannot turn themselves into a photograph and slide themselves under the door like Dr. Bombay on *Bewitched!* A ghost's energy usually respects physical objects like a door—not through them. There must be some basic level of physics to this all—or should I say, metaphysics?

"This doorknob turned and actually came off, while the girls were sitting here watching TV—they're kids, so they were a little bit scared that night," Beth continued. Doors aren't the only form of entry that the ghosts use in the house. They also seem to be using the windows as well! Beth went on to tell us about what she and her boyfriend Scott found in one of the upstairs bedrooms when the house was first being renovated.

"The window in my daughter's bedroom had fallen into the room, not just fallen—it was a few feet in. There was a lot of work being done in the house and there was a lot of dust. The floors are dark wood, but there were no foot prints in the dust at all." Beth showed us how the storm window was taken out and deposited by "something" in the middle of the room. There were no footprints or ladder marks in the dirt outside the window. Things certainly come and go in that house!

Beth also showed me where something crashed into their French doors between the kitchen and dining room one day, creating a huge bang. The new doors were added with the renovation and blocked the previous flow to the back part of the original house. The problem was, someone forgot to tell the ghosts. Beth has since left the doors open.

Ghost activity is usually at its highest when the building has new owners. The previous owners may have experienced very little, but the change of ownership is like an alarm clock for the paranormal!

Beth had her first experience with the ghosts when she had men working on the house, before she had even moved in.

"I've heard things—I thought people were upstairs. The very first time I came when workmen were here, I came to the front door. Very frequently, late in the afternoon while the painters were here, somebody would take the van and go get coffee. One of the times when that happened, had walked in the door and walked upstairs to the guy using the bathroom who didn't have the door closed, so what I came to do was announce myself, 'Hi guys I'm here," as I would come up the steps. One of the days I walked in the door and I said, 'Hi guys I'm here,' because I could hear the movement and stuff upstairs, figuring that somebody had gone out to get coffee. I walked upstairs and nobody was there. It stopped. Everything stopped, I went up to the third floor and there was nobody there.

I came down the stairs so fast that I don't remember even touching the steps! That was my first time anything ever happened. I flew out the door and went back to my office and said to the realtor, who was working with me, 'you have to go back and lock up the house.' Then I thought, we have to make peace with whatever is here."

Beth recalled that the sounds that she heard that day were perfectly clear. It sounded exactly like people walking around upstairs. I told Beth, that she should remember that she had moved in on the ghosts — not vice versa. People tend to forget that small fact! Beth agreed, and said, she realized that fact and came back with an open mind and just wanted to live with whomever else was in the house, in peace.

Before Beth bought the house, it was sitting unoccupied for a time between owners living there. I think the ghosts got used to having free run of their old house again and had to re-adjust when Beth's family moved in with them.

Instead of becoming full of fear when we think of ghosts, we should instead be full of amazement. Here are living souls, existing without their bodies and still going about business as usual. For the time, it all remains shrouded in mystery, but future science should someday be able to throw some light on the subject. Until then, you have myself and others who dabble in the mysterious field of parapsychology. We should remember to keep open minds on all things we do not fully understand. Human beings today, take such an old-world, backward view of the paranormal. One would think we were still dwelling in caves! Come on folks, television signals, cell phones, the internet, wireless everything—since when does not being able to see something make it impossible to exist?

The day we did the investigation of the Reeves house, I finally got to discover what was under that old trap door! Beth had opened it for us and we were able to look inside. Underneath the house were tunnels that formed a high crawlspace. About the only thing I could sense down there was all of the various air conditioning and heating duct work that now ran under the house. I starred down into the trap door, beyond the old wooden floor boards. There was nothing odd to report. No ghostly activity, no feeling of Underground Railway activity, no hidden bootleg whisky, not even a *Tell Tale Heart*. There was just an strange feeling around the closet, like something was *with us* as we were looking down through the floor boards. If Harriet Tubman had been here, we will probably never know for sure.

We made our way upstairs and the energy changed again. Beth and her boyfriend Scott showed us a hall closet that had a few ghosts of its own. Scott had been in the shower and heard cats meowing, like they were trapped. Beth and Scott traced the cries to their upstairs hall closet. Thinking their own had gotten locked inside they opened the door to let it out, but there was not a cat to be found and the cries stopped. They had let the cat out, they just did not realize it was a ghost cat!

I started sensing the name, "Emma" or "Emily." She was all over the second floor of the house. I learned later that John W. Reeve's wife was Emma L. Nott (1841-1904.) The name was very strong in one of the bedrooms. At the time I was thinking John's wife was Mahala, but that turned out to be a different John Reeves. Jim had given me the correct wife's name, Emma, shortly before I wrote this chapter. I only wish I knew who Emma was at the time, as I would have asked her some specific questions. On the other hand, it is much better to get correct names and validate them after the fact. If I had previously known her name, that could have stuck in my subconscious creating a false positive in the investigation.

I was sensing both a man and a woman. I asked them to identify themselves on the tape. They did not, but a man's voice says, "Why don't y'all go up to the third floor." Great, now I was channeling ghosts from Texas—I didn't know the power of my own transmitter!

I asked the ghosts when they lived in the house. Nothing was on the tape, but they gave me a date of 1821, which I think, referred to an earlier house on the property or nearby. As old as the Reeves home was, they were giving me the impression that I was standing in the "new" house. I asked if they were members of the Reeves family and again, there was no response on the tape.

At that point, only my psychic line was working. The EVP network seemed to be down! I sensed they wanted us to go to the third floor, maybe I was hearing the delayed response that appeared on the tape a few minutes earlier.

Beth told me when she first saw the house she fell in love with it. She pulled in front and didn't even want to look at any other house. She just told her realtor to give the people a deposit and pay what they were asking. If I had the money, I might have done the same, it is a beautiful house and in a quiet part of town.

We went up to the third floor and the energy changed yet another time. Now I was sensing a child. The adult ghosts did not follow me up the chairs. I asked the rest of my (living) group to allow me a few minutes of quiet. I sat in one of the rooms that I felt was the most active. I could sensed a ball of energy around a small rocker in the corner by the window. It was "little" energy, that of a child. The child immediately recognized that I could "see" her and told me her name was "Ginny" or "Jenny." It was difficult to understand her, she seemed very young. Even hundred-year-old ghosts of children will continue to speak in their previous manner from when they last lived. It is part of their earthly energy that they have refused to shed. I went with the name Ginny for the time being.

I told Beth that the girl was sitting in the chair right next to me. Beth bought the chair when she was 21 from an old estate sale and kept it with her everywhere she moved. Beth loves the chair and often comes upstairs to sit in it.

Ginny had suffered from a childhood illness and was having trouble "breathing." She was not really breathing. Again, the illness was a residual energy from her life. She was talking about an old doll she plays with in a trunk. Holding the dolls close to her chest made her feel better, she told me. Beth confirmed that her daughter's dolls were in another room in the attic in an old trunk.

A ghostly playmate was mentioned as coming to see Ginny from down the road. She also said the word "sassafras" and I am not sure if she was referring to a tree on the property or not. I don't think there were any Sassafras trees nearby. Perhaps the child just liked the way the word rolled off her tongue. Can you picture me standing there, all serious, channeling a little kid who is saying whatever nonsense comes in to her head?

Ginny told us her "Daddy lived here, but he's gone." I think she meant he had left the house, possibly after she had died. I did not feel she had an attachment to a mother figure, other than Beth. While I was talking to the child, I began to see imagery of beautiful gardens from the past. The Reeves family were mostly farmers, so this could have been how it looked in the old days around the house.

Beth's old cat was a favorite of Ginny's, but she "gets knots," she told me.

"She does, she does get knots," Beth confirmed. "This is the room that the cat sleeps in."

Ginny continued to talk about the cat and on the tape said, "He wants to come in." The cat was outside at the time. She also told me the cat is afraid of the mouse.

Jenny's favorite spot—an old rocker on the third floor (Photo by Sandra Bemis)

"He *was* afraid of the mouse!" Beth recalled the story of seeing a mouse in the kitchen, and bringing her cat into the room to get it, except the cat turned out to be a—excuse the pun—scardy cat and almost clawed Beth's face as she tried to get away from the mouse! Ginny found the entire thing very amusing, but still loved the old cat.

It also seems the young ghost, like her living counterparts, has entered the computer age early. "She plays with the computer up here, so if you are ever typing and there are some phantom letters on there you know it's her with the keys," I told Beth, "she presses them."

She also sends *me* emails in the middle of the night!

"That's in my daughters computer in the room we were just in," Beth confirmed.

"Your daughter's computer has acted up?"

"Yes, yes! She does!" Beth exclaimed.

"She likes the music on the computer and she plays around with that," Ginny wanted me to tell Beth.

"She does and I yell at her all the time to turn the computer off, when she leaves the house, because it's wasting energy. She swears to me that she turns it off and when I come home it's on and her iTunes™ play list is on!"

The ghost also finds it necessary to take a bath once in a while. "She always plays with the water in my daughter's bathroom!"

The little girl in the attic seemed to be very content staying right where she is. She knew Beth was selling the house and moving to smaller quarters now that her girls are grown. She did not say anything about going along with Beth to the next house. I think Ginny has seen many people come and go in her stay at the Reeves house.

She started to talk about a barn nearby and going to pet the horses, the living horses, that is. I assumed she meant the horse and carriage barn nearby.

The EMF meter spiked to 1.9 on the chair and Sandy kept clocking about 0.6 when she would hold the meter near my side. The rest of the house had a constant reading of zero to 0.2.

Ginny went on and on and told Beth her daughter should not talk on the phone when she walks down the stairs, because she saw Beth's daughter fall.

"She did fall down the stairs, and she was talking on the cell phone and I yelled at her!" Ghosts do watch us and they must be amused by what they see. She called Beth's daughter Danielle, "Nell" and says she sometimes sleeps in her room.

"She plays with the TV in my daughter's room," Beth added. The ghost was very fond of this family. She also wanted to tell them about the man downstairs, who was another ghost.

Ginny went on and on about "purple shoes" that she "loves to wear." Beth said neither she or her daughters owned any purple shoes. It was an odd thing for the child to say we all thought. Was she sneaking into someone else's home and looking for purple shoes? We told Ginny that purple shoes are not in fashion anymore.

She told us she misses her swing and Beth confirmed the old swing, had been taken down in the backyard about a year ago.

While she was telling me about the swing, she also asked about the "lady who worried about the roses." Beth told me a previous owner had seen the ad for the house being for sale, that her daughter had placed in a Philadelphia paper. The woman called and specifically asked if the big rose bushes were still alive in front of the house. Ginny remembered the woman fondly.

At this point on the tape a deep-voiced man's voice is heard as an EVP saying, "Here they come!" Right after that the quiet background hiss becomes populated with a cacophony of sounds and voices. It started to sound like some other places in town I had investigated. Noisy people were yapping about something, but I could not make out what they were saying. A ghost fan club?

We wrapped up and I said goodbye to Ginny and told Beth I would do my best to find out who she belong to.

As I wrote this article, I consulted with Jim Campbell to put together a Reeves family tree. As Jim read off names and dates, I kept hoping for a Ginny Reeves or a Virginia Reeves, but there was none. Was Ginny a servant's daughter? There was so much history surrounding this house.

The great thing about this property is that it was in the same family for so many years. There is ancestor named John Reeves who is listed as having bought all of this land in 1699 from the West New Jersey Society. I was told by the historians that the Reeves farm was at one time several hundred acres.

History is a little bit cloudy when it comes to this property. I think that over the years more than one Reeves family had lived in the house. Since Civil War veteran Captain John W. Reeves was only born in 1840, and Beth Bozzelli has traced the house on the property back to about 1837, I think it is safe to assume that John W. Reeves' ancestors had built the first house on the "Old Reeves Farm," as it was called for many years.

Janet Eldredge Vance had told me that her grandmother was a Reeves and she wold often visit her "Uncle Johnny" at this home on Stevens Street. As I mentioned earlier, speaking with Janet Vance was like a trip through Cape May history. She has incredible recall of people and places in town, even having left West Cape May and moved to Court House in 1938! She is the daughter of Judge Henry H. Eldredge whose mother was a Reeves.

With Jim Campbell's assistance, I started to piece together the Reeves family tree. Janet Vance's grandmother was Emma Julie Reeves (1848-1922.) Emma was the daughter of Andrew H. Reeves (1805-1875) and the granddaughter of Abijah Reeves (1750-1822.) Abijah Reeves was an early settler in Cape May along with his brothers. In addition to Andrew, he had another son Joshua Hand Reeves (1808-1855.) Joshua was the father of John W. Reeves. So, I told Janet when I called her back, her "Uncle Johnny" was actually her cousin Johnny. She told me in those days, with such a large family, even older cousins were referred to as "Aunt" and "Uncle." The amazing thing was I actually was talking to someone who remembered John Reeves and the house!

This little exercise in genealogy did jar my memory however. The name "Andrew H. Reeves" sounded so familiar—then I remembered why. A few years ago, when I was first in the Reeves homestead, I was doing a channeling session in the living room. As you have read in previous chapters, when I channel I can pull in small crowds of the dead from neighboring houses or even off the street. I must be the P. T. Barnum of the ghost circuit!

Several ghosts had come through the house that evening and told me they were buried nearby. Not in the yard, but somewhere across the road. I had never heard of any burial grounds in South Cape May, which was across Sunset Avenue, but maybe they were buried, early, somewhere in West Cape May before the days of Cold Spring Church's burial ground, and that *would* be early!

The spirits were very old and felt very learned as well. From what I gathered, they may have been early settlers or even older Native American Indians, who had summered on the peninsula. I had encountered several spirits of Native Americans in this region of Cape May and also over on Higbee Beach. That story follows this chapter. I made a note of the visitation and, while finding it fascinating, it had nothing to do with the house, I thought. I filed the information away in my archives.

Some time later, while reading Jeffrey M. Dorwart's great book, *Cape May County, New Jersey: The Making of an American Resort Community,* I came across a reference to old Indian graves being found in West Cape May. It mentioned an article found in the *Cape May Star and Wave* back in the 1930s about construction workers unearthing Indian burial mounds. I wanted to find out exactly where the graves were found, but he only mentioned "Cape May Gardens," a new development at the time.

Off I went to the West Cape May Borough Hall fresh with the information and excitedly questioned the ladies behind the counter concerning the whereabouts of Cape May Gardens and the old Indian burial ground. If their the counter was a door, it would have been slammed in my face. They were completely apathetic to my cause, and denied the fact that there were ever any Indian burial grounds in this part of Cape May. I tried to tell them about the *Star and Wave* article, but they just glared at me like I was crazy. Talk about a cold spot!

To Court House I went and into the microfilm archives of the old *Cape May Star and Wave* I dug. There it was, the exact date Dorwart had mentioned. A section of the original article appears on the following page with the text reproduced next to it.

The Cape May Star and Wave:

"For many years, so many that the origin is obscured in mystery, a mound of earth was the center of the William H. Reeves homestead and farm. In the memory of the oldest residents in the vicinity the mound was there. In the form of a circle, the larger mound was topped by a lone grave shaped one and the whole was many years ago surrounded by a small low fence which preserved its sanctity.

The first recorded owner of this tracts was the father of Andrew H. Reeves, who may have been one of those who came into this county in 1772. As recorded by the Hon. Lewis T. Steven's History of Cape May County, Abijah Reeves with his brothers, Adonijah and Abraham came here in 1772. One of these three, probably Abijah was the first owner and his descendents were Andrew and William in line. At any rate, this great grandfather of Mrs. Marcus Scull, the daughter of William H. Reeves, and who played about the old farm as a child, handed down the information that the mounds were there when he took possession, and that no one knew who lay buried there.

Hundreds of Indian relics, arrow heads, tomahawks, mortars and the like have been found on the farm and near these mounds.

There seems to be an established legend that there were from four to six bodies in the little burial plot, but when the workman last Monday, not knowing the significance because the fence has long since decayed and disappeared, caused the big scoop of the shovel to dig the earth up, they discovered but three remains.

Two skulls and other bones could be identified as belonging to three human bodies, but even the craniums were deteriorated to a great extent showing the great time they had line in the earth. The teeth of the skulls were carefully examined by the men who reported that while cavities in the teeth were evident there were no indications that any of them had been filled. This fact gave rise to the belief that they might be

From the Cape May Star and Wave
1937 Volume 71, Number 8

those of Indians, but as no Indian relics were dug up at the time, that idea has given place to a conjecture that some of the earliest settlers had been unearthed from what their friends had believed would be their last resting place.

The bones lay about four feet beneath the surface and the work men say that the next cut made by the shovel was at a shallower depth so that the other bodies, if there were any, had been passed over."

At the time of this writing, I have not yet been able to determine the exact size of the "Old Reeves Farm." It seems all that is left is Bath Bozzelli's home and her small two-acre lot. The article mentions South Cape May being filled in. This would have been across the street near what today, the bird sanctuary. Walt Campbell told me they had tried to develop what was left of old South Cape May over the years, but it was too marshy and things would sink in the mud.

As I mentioned earlier, I asked Jim Campbell if there was ever a Ginny Reeves or a Virginia Reeves. Unfortunately, Janet Vance's Uncle Johnny had three sons, not one daughter.

"Leroy, Carl and Andrew," Jim read off John's next of kin to me over the phone. None of the sons had a daughter named Ginny either.

I had remembered Janet Vance mentioning Winchester Reeves had lived in the house. "What about John's son Winchester?" I inquired to Jim.

"Winchester, there's no Winchester Reeves listed," he said. Another dead end. "Wait a minute, there is a "Samuel Winchester Reeves, two of them actually," he continued, "Samuel Winchester Reeves, born 1839, died 1904, Philadelphia, son of Andrew H. Reeves.

Well that worked. But he was not John's son, so it really did not work. He was John's first cousin.

"No Ginny anywhere in the family?" I asked Jim.

"No, no Ginny or Virginia," he told me as he combed through his old cemetery records from Cold Spring, "There is a Jenny Reeves."

Jenny? Why hadn't he mentioned this before? I could not find a Ginny or a Jenny Reeves in any of the old census records.

"She was the daughter of Samuel Winchester Reeves," he told me. "When was she born?"

"1875..." he replied and before I could even get the next question out, he answered it for me, "and she died in 1877 at the age of three."

A three-year-old named Jenny Reeves. BINGO! I found my Ginny who was now, really, *Jenny*.

On Janet's lead, I started checking Samuel Winchester Reeves. He was the oldest son of Andrew H. Reeves. According to the *Star and Wave* article, Andrew owned the house and farm first. He would have probably left it to his oldest son, Samuel Winchester. Samuel Winchester died in Philadelphia, but had two children in Cape May, Samuel Winchester, Jr., and Jenny M. Reeves. Did his family share the house with John W. Reeves?

I checked the old maps I had in my collection and found something strange. On the 1850 Numan Map, J. Reeves (John's father Joshua Hand Reeves) is shown living further up on Stevens Street and then on the Swain's 1877 map John is living on Broadway and Fourth, across the street from the Eldredge House (see opposite map.) Someone else was in the house when Jenny M. Reeves was born, and it might have been her father Samuel.

Janet Vance remembers John at the Reeves Homestead when she was young, and she was born in 1912, so that puts him in the house around that year.

Samuel Winchester Reeves lost his wife Tryphena in 1900. She died in Cape May. Four years later he died in Philadelphia. The Reeves are listed as living in Philadelphia on the 1880 census, but Samuel Jr., and Jenny M. Reeves were born in Cape May. Two other daughters, Lottie B. Reeves 1873 and *another* Jenny—Jenny W. Reeves, born in 1880 are listed as being born in Pennsylvania. Janet Vance remembered two daughters, but not a Jenny. That would have been way before her time. The second girl named Jenny may have gone by a middle name.

Being a lawyer, Samuel Winchester Reeves probably did business in Philadelphia and had a second home there. Or he retired to Cape May after his father Andrew passed. After Samuel died in 1904, the house may have passed to Captain John W. Reeves. I thought it was always home to the Captain, but I was incorrect. Only a title search on the property can truly reveal the chain of ownership. Unfortunately, the ghosts come first, and the historical research, always a favorite past time of mine, must follow second.

For now, all the evidence points to Jenny M. Reeves as the ghost.

Now about those purple shoes...

I received a frantic call from Beth Bozzelli the day after I visited her home and did the investigation. She had been telling her daughter Lauren about my findings. When she got to the part with the purple shoes, the phone went silent.

"Mom, my purple jellies are in the trunk in the attic — the ones that I wore when I was three!" Lauren reminded her mother.

Beth was blown away. She had forgotten that when Lauren was about three or four, everything had to be purple, including her purple jelly shoes — which she kept to

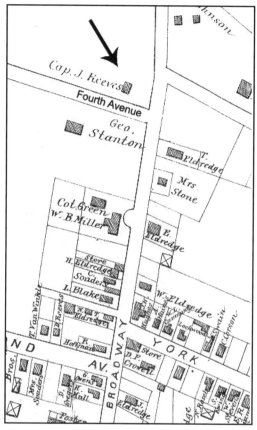

Swain's 1877 Map — showing Capt. John Reeves' West Cape May home in 1877.

this day in the trunk in the attic along with the dolls that Jenny loved to play with!

Beth was very open minded before. Now she was a believer!

I think I made her day when it was my turn to place the frantic call to her and let her know I found Ginny, I mean — Jenny.

The old Reeves Homestead will soon change ownership once again. Maybe someday I will also be on that honorable list. Hmm — I better get rid of my purple shoes.

The Ghosts of Higbee Beach

The Ghosts of Higbee Beach
THE DEAD SEE
On the Bay in Cape May

THERE have been reports of strange sightings on Higbee Beach for many years. However, in the past decade most of those reports had more to do with naked sunbathers and lewd behavior than with ghosts. There *were* paranormal sightings, but they were less frequent. I must admit that for someone who had spent summers in Cape May since the late 1960s, I had never once set foot on Higbee Beach until Summer of 2005. Was I missing out on a great Cape May experience!

According to historical accounts the area that is now Higbee Beach and the adjoining inlands were from Cape May's earliest civilized times farm land. In Robert C. Alexander's 1956 edition of *Ho! For Cape Island!* Alexander mentions that Thomas and Rhoda Forrest owned a tavern, from 1807–1823, on the site where Higbee would later build his hotel. Historian Jim Campbell told me that the area's namesake, Joseph Smith Higbee (1796–1872), purchased the farmland and a hotel on the property around the year 1823. The hotel was called The Hermitage.

Higbee, and his younger brother Thomas Harris Higbee (1804–1879) continued its operation as a lodging place for Delaware Bay pilots for many years. In discussing the old Hermitage, Jim Campbell feels that the Higbees added to an existing hotel instead of building it from scratch. I would surmise they might have expanded the Forrest's tavern into bigger accommodations for guests. Contrary to local legend, the Higbee brothers did not live in the old "Higbee Hotel." They instead lived in a house on Bayshore Road, near Higbee Beach, that still stands today.

In 1916, the Wilson family lived in the old Higbee hotel and the Wilson's daughter Letitia "Tisch" Fleischauer gave Jim a complete oral history, before she died in February of 2000 a the age of 94.

The Hermitage Hotel was added onto over the years, with the original structure being built without any nails, an interesting feat in those days! Tisch Fleischauer also told Jim that Tom Higbee ran the hotel while his brother Joseph worked as a Delaware Bay pilot.

In the Higbee's day a lantern was always kept in the top window of the hotel, which sat about two hundred yards back from the beach near where the Higbee's Beach parking lot is now located, near the canal. Passing pilots would see the lantern in the window of the hotel which beckoned those in need of nightly lodging.

During the Higbee's ownership of the old hotel, another famous Cape May family joined the mix. Amanda Miller and her sister Wilhelmina came to work at the hotel under Thomas Higbee. Miller eventually married another Delaware Bay pilot, Douglas Gregory who would go on to build what is today The Queen Victoria Bed and Breakfast. As I was researching the families for this article, I found the two families had close ties.

When Amanda Miller Gregory had her first daughter on November 25, 1861, she named her Martha Marie Antoinette Gregory after Thomas and Joseph Higbee's infant sister, Marie Antoinette Higbee, who died around 1802, and the Higbee's mother Martha Howell Higbee, who died in 1808 in Bridgeton. When Amanda Gregory had her son on August 28th 1863, she named him Joseph Smith Higbee Gregory in homage to Joseph Higbee. It was interesting to note that she did not name her children for either her family or her husband's family. Sadly, Amanda Gregory died on February 28, 1869 at the age of 25 and Etta, as her daughter Martha was called, was raised by her "Uncle Tom" Higbee. Gregory's parents raised Gregory's son Joseph since Douglas Gregory was away at sea working as a Delaware Bay pilot most of the time.

Joseph Higbee died in 1872, followed by his brother Thomas in 1879. Tom Higbee left his entire estate to Etta Gregory. In his will, he

asked to be buried near the hotel in a grave lined with brick and flagstone. The grave was then sealed shut with a large marble slab with Higbee's information etched into it. Higbee was not allowed to rest undisturbed as he had planned, however. In 1935, upon her death, Etta Gregory's will instructed that her "Uncle Tom" be disinterred and buried along with her, next to the Gregory plot in the Cold Spring Cemetery. The grave was to be filled with sand taken from Higbee's Beach. The Higbee and Gregory plots can still be found today sitting quietly on the far right side of the old brick church. Someone however, is not at rest on Higbee's Beach, and this ghost hunter encountered that someone and he had *lots* of company!

Searching for the old ruins of Higbee's Hotel and attempting to explore the myriad of nature paths through Higbee's Beach State Park turned out to be a futile effort, at least on the historical front. I should have heeded Jim Campbell's words, "You can't find the ruins in the summer. You have to wait for the winter when the foliage dies back — otherwise the place is full of poison ivy, ticks and mosquitoes." I felt like the cowardly lion in *The Wizard of Oz,* and I should be skipping with my companions through the old woods chanting, "Poison ivy and mosquitoes and ticks — OH MY!"

I though it would be a wonderful summer's journey into the natural wilds of the bayside. BIG mistake. Did I mention that the paths

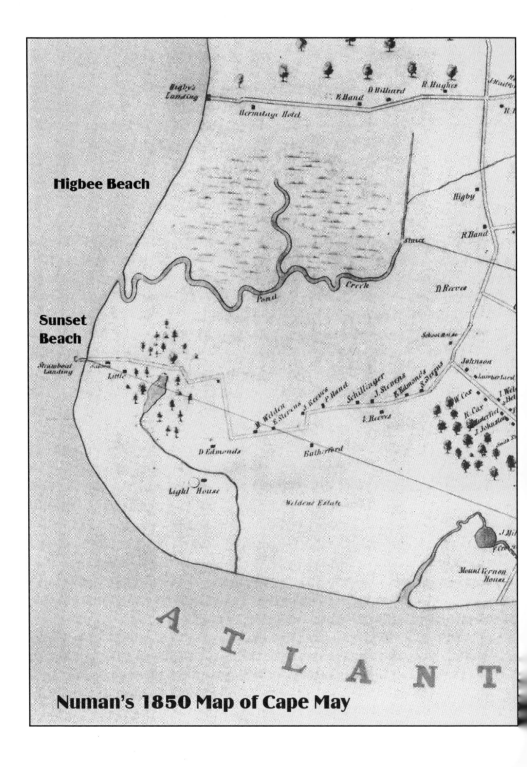

going up the dunes were laced with strands of *rusty* old *barbed wire* fencing? That was *before* droves of mosquitoes started to use my friend Kathy's neck as a landing strip and the ticks and poison ivy chose my partner Willy to assault. I, being the most paranoid of the group, carefully maneuvered around anything with three leaves or wings that came into our path.

Speaking of paths, you would think in a state park the paths would be better tended. Most of the paths we found looked as if people had made them 100 years ago! There were few markers and some paths simply disappeared into the foliage leaving the hiker with no option but to turn back and start again. The only redeeming thing about the isolated nature of the Higbee woods was that the dead did not mind being so isolated—they seemed to enjoy being in the middle of nowhere.

As we meandered down one winding path, we encountered a newt or lizard sunning itself on a dead tree. The cute little reptile just stood there and seemed to give us a grin as we moved by. It was watching us and then turned away to watch something else in our path. My psychic radar came on and I sensed a ghost—finally.

The image of a spirit of a young girl popped into my head. She had long blond hair à la *Alice in Wonderland*. She was on one side of us in the woods and then vanished and reappeared on the other side of us. She seemed well dressed in period clothing from long ago. The young girl came and went as if she were playing a game of hide and seek with us. Another example of a lost child's ghost lurking about Cape May.

Jim Campbell told me that in the old 1870 and 1880 censuses in Cape May, everyone who had died in the year prior to the census was also listed. Almost 40% of the dead were children under ten years of age. This is certainly a big reason why Cape May is a *paranormal playground* for so many souls of children.

"Alice," as I will call her, because I could not keep her attention long enough to gather information psychically, seemed to be wandering aimlessly, further back into the woods. The most striking thing about this ghost's appearance was her brilliant blond hair. It glistened like pure energy.

My psychic instincts gave me the feeling that she was tied to the old Town Bank settlement that had existed further up the coast. It was where the first settlers of Cape May lived in the 1600s and mid 1700s. Most of the area is now under water, including the old graveyard and all of its bodies!

We decided not to pursue Alice, as the path was disappearing and Kathy wondered aloud if the newt we had encountered at the beginning of the path was indeed some kind of *Cheshire Cat-like* harbinger, letting us know in its own way we were headed for a *dead* end. It was amusing to think so at least. I could see how one could become lost in the maze of bramble and brush. My common sense kicked, in and I turned the group back to civilization.

We returned to high ground overlooking the bay and beach when I started receiving imagery of an older man wearing black boots with buckles on them. It was the second time I had received such a mental image. I had been to Higbee briefly a few weeks earlier to get the feel of the place, and the ghostly man had appeared to me at that time as well. A quick meditation would help to make a connection. I sat comfortably in the sand and focused on the sounds of the surf.

As I sat on the high dunes listening to the surf below, I closed my eyes and started to meditate. Higbee Beach is a great place to relax and meditate. A man walked toward me in my psychic radar. I could see his boots, but the rest of his image was muddled. I could sense he knew the place as he gave me the impression, psychically, that I was in *his* space. He seemed to be dragging a long log or piece of drift wood behind him. I felt he was using it for firewood. Ghosts will carry physical objects with them. These are not objects in our physical plane but reflections of objects from another plane of existence. I do not understand how it works, but ghosts stay busy doing tasks that involve things that they can manipulate. A ghost may cause a chair to move or a pen to roll off a table, but you will usually not see that same pen writing a letter. However, one might catch a glimpse of an apparition with a pen of its own—from its own time, like the firewood that this man was dragging. Was this the ghost of one of the Higbees? Many

people over the years have spotted a man's ghost walking along the dark paths at Higbee Beach. Most assumed it was "old man" Higbee.

From the earliest times a steamship landing existed at Higbee's Beach when the area was referred to as "the cove." It was a busy place and considering all the shipwrecks the bayside saw over the years, there is more than a good chance this phantom man is a sailor who may have been lost at sea. As strong a presence as the man was, the most interesting spirits I encountered at Higbee's Beach were not local sailors, but Native American Indians.

We took a path back into the woods after encountering the ghost of the man with black boots. This time we headed towards Davy's Lake, a man-made body of water left behind from Higbee's past life as a sand mining area. Once again the paths started twisting and turning and getting narrower with each turn. I began to feel a complete change of energy. There was a very old energy to the part of the woods we had just entered. Thoughts started to run through my mind of getting lost, but in Cape May that is pretty hard to do. Eventually you will come to water whichever direction you go!

The tree cover created an eerie darkness even though it was a bright, sunny day and only about 2 PM. I stopped the group and looked around. I had heard someone talking, several people—adult men. It is not uncommon to find trail hikers at Higbee, so I waited to see in which direction they were coming. No one was in sight and the voices stopped. As a matter of fact, all the sounds had stopped. I commented to Kathy and Willy that not a single bird could be heard chirping. No insect noises, no birds, no surf sounds, silence.

Suddenly, out of nowhere a man's ghostly voice said to me, "This is sacred ground." It felt like someone had come up behind us and deliberately tried to startle us. I turned to look and realized no one else had heard the voice. The words "sacred ground" immediately made me realize I was encountering a Native American spirit. I tried to respond with a greeting from my mind. There were two men, both American Indians—they surrounded us with their energy, as if they could spread themselves out in space. Kathy asked me what tribe they were from and the response before I could ask was, "Delaware." The Kechemeches were a tribe of Lenni Lenape Indians who were descended from the Delaware tribe. I was surprised the spirits did not identify themselves as Kechemeches. Perhaps they were even older and had resided on the peninsula in the summertime like the other tribes had done, coming to Cape May to fish and bathe. Native Americans were truly Cape May's original tourists.

I tried to focus on the men's energies to ask questions, but it was too strong and was coming at me quickly and not letting my energy send an exchange of communication back. I tried to ask them if they were referring to the land in such a manner because they once owned it and perhaps it was an Indian burial ground. They had already put the answer back into my mind before I could finish the question.

"No one owns the land," was the response—short and profound.

Trying not to be disrespectful, but realizing the mosquitoes (who thought they *did* own the place) were having us for lunch, I decided to take the group back to civilization. The path ahead of us had literally disappeared from site and we even found the return trip challenging. I am not against a nature walk, but the paths through Higbee's seem to have a mind of their own and I am not good at getting lost!

Once back on the beach, we walked through the warm surf to try to sooth our mosquito and tick attacked limbs. We stopped by a strand of old wind-blown dead trees that covers part of the high bluff facing. At the foot of the bluff is a Y shaped tree inscribed with the words "Voodoo Tree." Appropriately and artistically carved into the opposite side of the tree is the face of a Native American Indian. I wonder how many others have encountered the same lost world that looms back within the boundaries of Higbee Beach?

As I mentioned in the introduction, I recently returned to Higbee Beach, but decide to enter from the Sunset Beach side, instead of the New England Road entrance a few miles north. Walking along that part of Higbee, I finally found Davy's Lake. We had been nowhere near it when we were foraging through the woods at the other end of Higbee Beach a few years ago. This entire strip of beach is a fantastic walk. I think it would be absolutely magical to transverse the entire stretch, at night, under the stars. I am sure one would not be walking alone on Higbee Beach at night. A paranormal encounter or two would probably be a very strong possibility.

Higbee Beach is now part of the State of New Jersey's Higbee Beach Wildlife Management Area. It is a 1000+ acre of wildlife preserve featuring all kinds of migratory animals. It also has a few migratory ghosts lurking about!

I have been in some of the most haunted houses around, but there is something about being so alone with nature, so isolated from civilization, so smothered by ghosts, that gives Higbee Beach my nod as one of the most haunted and chilling places in town—if you happen to be *looking* for ghosts. And if you should do your ghost hunting in the summer months, remember to come well prepared. Dress wisely and bring a can of insect repellent.

Haunted houses may make your blood run cold, but at least you will still have it. Haunted forests in the height of summer, on the other hand, may just leave you short a pint or two. Especially if you happen to get lost in the woods, or stumble into old man Higbee's empty, open grave. Happy hunting.

Ghosts of the Lighthouse

BENEATH THE RAYS OF THE CIRCLING LIGHT
DEAD SOULS WANDER THROUGH THE NIGHT

Cape May Point

AS A regular visitor to Cape May, I rarely get to the lighthouse. Once I park in town I generally move within walking distance of my car. In 2006, for the first time, I actually walked up all 199 stairs of the old lighthouse to take in the fantastic view that 145 feet above the surf had to offer. The lighthouse at Cape May Point is truly one of the rare gems of the Cape. It also has its share of ghosts roaming around the grounds and these "moving targets" made it especially difficult for this ghost investigator to seek them out.

Cape May Point is surrounded by the turbulent waters, dangerous shoals and ever changing sandbars where the Delaware Bay and Atlantic currents collide. It is these factors that have attributed to many shipwrecks and drownings over Cape May's long history as a seaside resort community.

When I walk through the *Cape May Diamond* studded sands of the Point, I usually sense entities from these past tragedies. On that particular trip in 2006 however, I decided to focus my attention on the venerable beacon that has become a well known Cape May landmark.

Built in 1859 to replace two earlier incarnations, the 157 foot tall sentinel known as the Cape May lighthouse has been warning ships away from the treacherous shoals at the tip of southern New Jersey for almost 150 years. It has survived much longer than its two predecessors that were built in 1823 and 1847 which eventually surrendered to the raging sea. The lighthouse sees tens of thousands of visitors each year, and the middle of summer is generally a bad time to try to conduct a quiet ghost investigation.

Now under the direction and care of The Mid-Atlantic Center for the Arts (MAC,) the lighthouse has, after years of restoration, returned to its former grandeur. A few former lightkeepers and their families—now dead—are also enjoying the views from above. Except they are not watching from Heaven. It's the top of the old light. Some ghosts seem to be guided by their old paths and former duties on Earth. The ghosts of the light certainly appear to be working. Does the light still act as some sort of a beacon for the dead as well as the living?

Since that first climb up the lighthouse steps, I have visited the lighthouse many more times. As part of our latest ghost tour, *Ghosts of the Lighthouse*, the old sentinel has become one of my more frequent stops. I will tell you this, it is much more pleasant to climb 199 steps in cooler weather! At the time of my first visit however, I was writing my *Exit Zero Ghost Writer* column and needed to meet a press deadline, which happened to be in the *dead of summer*. It was hot and humid, the mosquitoes could have carried away young children.

I arrived at 8:15 PM, after the light had closed to tourists for the day. I had arranged to meet the current "keeper of the light," Rich Chimiengo, who managed the lighthouse and gave tours there for MAC. Rich unlocked the large iron gate and proceeded to tell the history of the old light. He was a font of information and showed us a myriad of historical details in the architecture.

As we began to ascend the old spiral staircase, I felt rather like Julie Harris in the 1963 horror classic *The Haunting*. In that classic haunted house movie, Harris' character ascends a great spiral staircase in the old library, slowly winding her way up to the top of the library's stone tower. Each step she takes loosens the bolts holding the spiral staircase to the wall—a little further—causing the iron stairs to twist and wobble and giving the viewer a really bad case of vertigo! Luckily, the lighthouse's spiral staircase was firm and secure—but I

A ghost's eye view from one of the lighthouse landings.

could not get the image of that movie out of my mind all the while I slowly moved towards the top.

As I sat in my office in February of 2008 to complete this chapter of Book 3, I had remembered running a tape of the 2006 visit to the lighthouse, but had not seen it in about two years, it was misplaced. I had been slowly uploading all of my old investigation tapes into Adobe Audition® and scanning them for EVPs. This is an extremely time-consuming process. One needs to have the patience to sit and listen to every silent portion of the tape and mentally scan for anything that sounds like a voice. Once an EVP is found, the process of cleaning up the segment of the recording begins. Hiss reduction is applied and sometimes noise reduction and filters. The most important thing is not to over do it on the filtering or the EVP can be distorted and its meaning skewed.

I stood up and went to my stacks of tapes towering over my desk in order to review the tape for the writing of this chapter. The lighthouse tape was now on top of the pile. It was not around for two years and now it was staring me in the face. Someone was trying to help me get this book done. If only I could find a good ghost typist!

The tape of the lighthouse continued to offer up a bevy of ghostly voices, but very few made sense. Were the ghosts talking about us rather than to us?

I stopped on the first landing (there are six) to catch my breath and gaze out the small window. My partner Willy and I started two different tape recorders to try to capture any EVPs. I stopped and focused my psychic senses upward in the lighthouse. I invited the ghosts, if any were present, to speak onto the tape. When we first reviewed the tapes later that night, *children's voices* were heard yelling in the background. The gates to the property were locked and we were the only three in the lighthouse at that point. The voices were high pitched and occurred quickly and then ceased. The words were inaudible and the timing of the EVPs did not match the questions I was asking. This was another example of how EVPs are more ghostly background noise than actual interactive conversation with a ghost. I believe I caught ghosts of children on tape, but they were not nearby and were not aware of my presence. As I mentioned, I had only uploaded the tape to my computer two years later and at that point I could hear quite a few voices in addition to the child's yells.

Rich discussed the history of the light with us as we ascended to each landing. Willy stayed one landing behind us to attempt to scoop up some EVPs with the cassette recorder. Since Rich and I continued a dialogue for most of the climb, having the tape recorder a distance away might pick up ghosts who were trailing us. It seemed to work.

When we first began to climb the steps a child's voice could be heard getting closer. It was now late, and we were inside the light. The park was closed around the lighthouse. The child's voice seemed to shout out words that had a wind-blown quality to them. As we moved up the steps, EVPs of several men and a woman could be heard talking. These voices also possessed a breathy quality.

One theory about how EVPs are created is that a ghost will use existing sound waves and manipulate them to turn random white noise into words and sentences. All of the EVPs recorded that July evening at the lighthouse had a breathy quality to them. Could the ghosts be using the normal air currents that flow through the tower as carrier waves? This, of course, was assuming they were *trying* to communicate with me. Most of the words were distant and would be classified as Class C EVPs. One would need headphones to hear most of these conversations and even with headphones on, the voices were for the most part, inaudible. Were the ghosts talking with each other? The child's voice was clearest and loudest, but even that faded into the background. Was the ghostly child passing close to the tape recorder as it ascended the steps to join the others?

At one point on the tape, a motherly voice shouts out, "careful!" This is followed by a child's voice replying from a distance away, "I can see the sidewalk." I took this to mean the ghostly child was looking down from the top of the light and the mother figure was closer to where we stood halfway up the stairs.

I stopped at each landing (so I would not become a ghost) to catch my breath. The air was close in the old tower, and the humidity made it twice as uncomfortable. This was quite a change from the typical winter investigations I did in Cape May where I was usually freezing in some basement, attic or unheated building. When I finally got to the watch room, the cool ocean breeze was pouring in through the exterior door and greeted me like an old friend. Willy called me out onto the catwalk to see the spectacular sunset and view.

I thought I would *die*.

Still out of breath, I now had my fear of heights to contend with. Vertigo anyone? I eased myself just far enough out of the doorway to see (part of) the great view. I tried to regain my sense of calm and balance and tried to reassure myself that the lighthouse was not actually moving, it was just my equilibrium that was being tortured!

There was an odd feeling that came over me at that point. Even though the catwalk is completely fenced in, I had a strange sensa-

Opposite: Vintage Cape May Postcard from 1908 by L.W. Blasius depicting strange goings on at the old light — some things never change.

tion of someone trying to climb through the fence, almost a feeling of someone jumping off. Luckily, the fence is secure and that is physically impossible, but I thought I would head back into the watch room and take in the view through the windows. If there was a ghost or two taking a high dive, I wanted no part of it!

All of the paranormal activity now shifted below me. I kept getting a mental picture of a woman in a long dress coming up the steps with a bucket. She kept walking endlessly in the image, never getting to any particular place. Was this a residual haunting? Just a tape loop playing over and over again? An image of a past event stuck in the ether that intuitives like me can sense?

I put out some psychic feelers, but felt my energy literally hitting a wall. In a small confined space so far above the ground, one will rarely find a ghost just hanging, out waiting to chat.

There were ghosts, but they were moving. Only twice more did I sense the woman on the stairs. This perfectly illustrates my theory: A house is only haunted if the ghost happens to be at home. Ghosts move, they interact with other ghosts in a communal way and like their living counter parts, they get bored staying in one place. They may visit the lighthouse or work in the lighthouse, but they do not stay in the lighthouse. Sorry.

The type of ghost you *do* find exclusively haunting one room of one particular dwelling is usually a soul who has died under traumatic circumstances and refuses to admit it is dead. They are stuck in one place and refuses to move, usually for fear of losing the last physical place connection that it had to life. Some disembodied souls may get agitated when other living beings move into what was once their space, but eventually they do cross over to Heaven. Probably out of sheer boredom. That type of ghostly personality is *not* at the lighthouse.

Most ghosts know they are dead and seem to like it that way. They must realize there are limitations to their existence and boundaries that they cannot cross, and that their interaction with the living is physically and mentally limited, but they still like where they are better than where they think Heaven may take them. Maybe it is the safe feeling of being comfortable with one's surroundings.

I slowly made my way down the spiral staircase, feeling the constantly curving inner wall of the lighthouse as I went along. It was like a trip back through time. I was picking up residual images of many different time periods that were trapped as psychic energy in the walls of the old sentinel. Residual energy is a cool thing, but not something I was looking to tap into at the time. The ghostly woman was on the move again—this time she was at ground level.

I told Rich Chimiengo that I thought the woman had been a lightkeeper, and that I found that odd since I thought all of Cape May's keepers had been men. I was wrong. The last keeper, Arabelle Palmer, took over the duties from her husband Harry after a heart attack had prevented him from continuing his post. "Belle" as she was called manned the light from 1933 until 1935 when she and Harry finally retired to a home on Washington Street where they spent the rest of their years in Cape May. Had Belle Palmer returned to her old post?

On the tape, a woman's voice says, "Remember Belle" at the exact time Rich talks about Arabelle's tenure as lightkeeper.

The woman I was seeing looked to be from an even older period of time. The dress did not appear in my mind as 1930s era. It looked more 1800s to me. Rich told me there were several light keepers wives who lived on the premises. Two identical dwellings had been built in 1859 at the base of the lighthouse in order to house the keepers and their families. Only one building survives today and is now the home of the State Park Ranger who lives full-time on the property. Is the ghostly lady of the light haunting the old light keeper's house? By the time we had finished that evening I did not want to disturb the Park Ranger to ask.

Rich had never encountered any ghostly activity in the lighthouse in his tenure as manager. He did tell me he would keep a sharp ear out for future activity! There have been few reports of anything paranormal happening at the lighthouse over the last few years. As I returned to ground level and went out doors to take a few pictures by the base of the lighthouse, the paranormal activity increased. Now there were all kinds of personalities in the ethers. More than I had sensed when I first arrived. Did the ghostly legions wait until sunset to take a nightly stroll or frolic in the surf?

I first sensed a man who seemed to have been in an accident as his head and shoulders were injured. I also sensed the same woman again, the lightkeeper, now holding the hands of two young children. Had one of the former lightkeeper's wives lost two children? Why would she stay behind with her children instead of crossing over to Heaven? There are a lot of unanswered mysteries about the ghost world that we have yet to discover.

We stood for a few moments, and I mentioned it would be a great shot if I had an old lantern to carry while walking up the stairs. Rich had just the thing in his office, but we were already heading outside. We decided to take a few shots of me holding the lantern up in the air at the base of the light house.

Big mistake.

Note to self: Never hold a lantern in the air, at night, in the summer, in a park, wearing shorts. I was soon covered in anything that could fly. Even bugs that didn't bite decided to land on me! Alek the photographer from *Exit Zero* who was with us that night made a comment that it made a really good scary picture of me. Of course I looked scared—I was being eaten alive!

This was a tough investigation.

I looked over toward the lightkeeper's house. There seemed to be paranormal activity moving to and from the beach. Were the old light keepers entertaining guests—I mean ghosts?

I decided to do one more EVP session on the ground floor of the lighthouse. I set the tape recorder down and focused my energies in the lighthouse. I asked for a name of who was with us. Voices could be heard, but nothing responded directly to my question. When I asked how many people were there with us at the light, the response sounded something like, "six forty nine" or "six for a yarn." I was inclined

The former Keeper's House sits beneath the old light.

to go with the latter interpretation and feel it meant six of them had come to hear our "story."

On that passage of the tape there were also a few disturbing EVPs. After a woman says "six for a yarn" a younger girl's voice cries out, "Help me please!" That is followed by a young boy's plea saying, "I want to go home." If one had witnessed this in a real life situation, the boy's moaning may not have seemed like anything more than a child's boredom. However, coupled with the girl's plea for help, I suddenly got a psychic flash that the children I have been "seeing" may have been orphaned ghosts that have been taken in by the lady of the light.

At this point I did not feel that it was Arabelle Palmer who was doing the haunting. I feel it is an earlier lightkeeper's wife, now acting as a surrogate mother as well. Can the children cross to Heaven or are they afraid to cross over? Are they being *kept* by the lady of the light or are they protected by her?

Rich had a copy of *Sentinel of the Jersey Cape* by John Bailey, a book that chronicles the story of the Cape May light. While he was telling me about the book and showing me some of the pictures, an EVP says, "Read the lines." Unfortunately, I did not hear that instruction at the time, and I do not remember which page we were reading when the EVP occurred, but it may have offered up a clue as to who is doing the haunting.

I made it a point to return several more times to the lighthouse with the focus of my investigation being on the grounds instead of inside the light. While I never made it to the ranger's house, I did get a good showing of ghostly inhabitants walking around near the base of the tower.

Some of the more colorful psychic images I received were that of privateers or pirates. Yes, even in Cape May we had pirates. Men who would wait for a ship to become stranded on the shoals and proceed to plunder its goods, sometimes at the demise of the ship's crew and passengers. Three of these rogues survive in the ghost realm today on Cape May Point. There are probably more, but these are the only three I could get on my psychic radar. They seemed to be dragging around boxes and crates. It appeared they were still hoarding pilfered goods on a ghostly level. They did not notice me, and one seemed to come at me and almost walk through me.

There was a ghostly man and his dog who were on some endless walk along the beach. Being a dog lover, I took comfort in the fact that they were still together. I guess one refuses to cross over to Heaven and the other is faithfully waiting for a group decision to go.

One of the most bizarre ghosts I encountered was more like a nightmare. It was late one night and I was walking around the grounds of the light and sensed the ghost of a child sitting in an inner tube and bouncing around the ground. Having owned one of those ride on giant rubber balls as a kid, I could see how a ghostly child would have fun bouncing on an old inner tube. I moved closer to the area, near the parking lot and focused my attention on the spot where the child was frolicking.

As I closed my eyes and asked the child her name, the image morphed into that of a woman in her 30s with long hair and smudged lipstick and a gash on her face. It took me a moment to react as a sense of dread overwhelmed me. Had she buried herself in the sand from the waste down or was I seeing her in a spot that used to be underwater? Perhaps at one time she was floating in a creek or tidal pool that occupied the same spot and now appears to be buried in the sand.

A split second later, she looked up at me and said in an almost drunken stupor, "I can't feel my legs! She began to laugh slowly at first and then faster and more maniacally as she began to bounce up and down revealing—she had no legs! The image was so grotesque I opened my eyes and moved away. What I thought was an innocent, ghostly child playing in an inner tube turned out to be a nightmarish drowning victim who must have lost her legs while swimming in the ocean. I don't know how or why and I did not stick around to ask. The feeling I got from her is that she *enjoyed* frightening people who were receptive like I was. Ghosts are just like people, some people enjoy playing practical jokes. Ghosts can take them to the next level.

Should you possess intuitive abilities, make sure you know what you are getting into before you go chasing after ghosts in the dark. Luckily this woman was just having a good laugh at my expense. Other ghosts can carry on a joke while following you home. Ghost hunting may seem like lots of fun, and it does have its rewards, but there is also a dark side to dealing with the dead. They can wreak havoc on those that are psychologically vulnerable. Just be careful.

After my encounter with the "inner tube lady," I wrapped it up at the lighthouse. If you want a good shot at encountering a ghost or two in Cape May, take my *Ghosts of the Lighthouse* trolley tour sponsored by MAC. The trolley leaves from Ocean Street at the end of the Washington Street Mall. The lighthouse is a magical experience at night, and the ghosts of the lighthouse will send a welcome chill down your spine on those hot summer nights!

I hope you have enjoyed reading my three *Ghosts of Cape May* books. This has been an amazing experience for me and I hope you have enjoyed the ride. Stay up to date with my writing and lectures by visiting my website www.craigmcmanus.com. I want to thank all of those involved in this ongoing project. I have never been big on goodbyes, so with that...

The Ghosts of Cape May would like to thank you for stopping by to hear their tales, and would like to invite you to take a refreshing, eternal dip with them...

...on the enchanted sands and in the cool surf of America's oldest *and most haunted* seaside resort.

Cape May, New Jersey — 1888
Where six feet under takes on a whole new meaning.